NIGHT OF THE LIVING DEAD COLORING BOOK

HORRID COLORING BOOKS VOL 1

WRITTEN BY

JORDAN COLTON

COVER BY
PATRICK KENDALL

EDITED BY
JULIE GREEN

ISBN: 0692545344
ISBN-13: 978-0692545348

DEDICATION

THIS IS DEDICATED FIRST AND FOREMOST TO MY MOM BECAUSE IF IT WASNT FOR HER I WOULDN'T BE HERE. SECOND TO KATHARYNE SHELTON AND THE COLORING MASTERMINDS WHO GAVE ME THE INSPRIATION TO GET THIS IDEA ROLLING, AND FINALLY GEORGE A ROMERO FOR INSPIRING SO MANY OF US HORROR FANATICS TO LOVE ZOMBIES AND THE UNDEAD. THIS WAS A VERY FUN PROJECT AND I HOPE YOU ENJOY COLORING THIS AS MUCH AS I HAVE HAD MAKING IT A REALITY!

ACKNOWLEDGEMENTS

I WISH TO ACKNOWLEDGE ALL OF MY HORROR FRIENDS THAT SHARE IN THE LOVE OF ALL THINGS SCARY. WITHOUT THEM I WOULDN'T LOVE IT AS MUCH AS I DO. THERE ARE SO MANY THAT ARE OUT THERE I CAN'T NAME ALL OF YOU.

TWO THAT NEED TO BE MENTIONED IN THIS BOOK ARE PATRICK KENDALL AND TRAVIS JONES. THEY ARE THE TWO BEST HORROR BUDDIES A GUY COULD EVER HAVE! EVERY YEAR AS WE GO TO MONSTERPALOOZA OR SPEND THE HALLOWEEN SEASON SACARING PEOPLE HALF TO DEATH ALWAYS BECOME AMAZINGLY MEMORABLE EXPEREIENCES WTH YOU TWO KNUCKLEHEADS!

THANK YOU ALSO TO MY FAMILY AND FRIENDS FOR BELIEVING IN ME AND ALLOWING ME TO BE CREATIVE. THEY STILL LOVE ME EVEN WHEN I COME HOME WIHT MY BRAND NEW HEARSE IN THE MIDDLE OF THE NIGHT. THAT WAS A GREAT WAY TO SCARE THE NEIGHBORS THE NEXT MORNING. SORRY MOM!

JORDAN COLTON PRESENTS
A HORRID COLORING BOOK

NIGHT
OF THE
LIVIING DEAD!

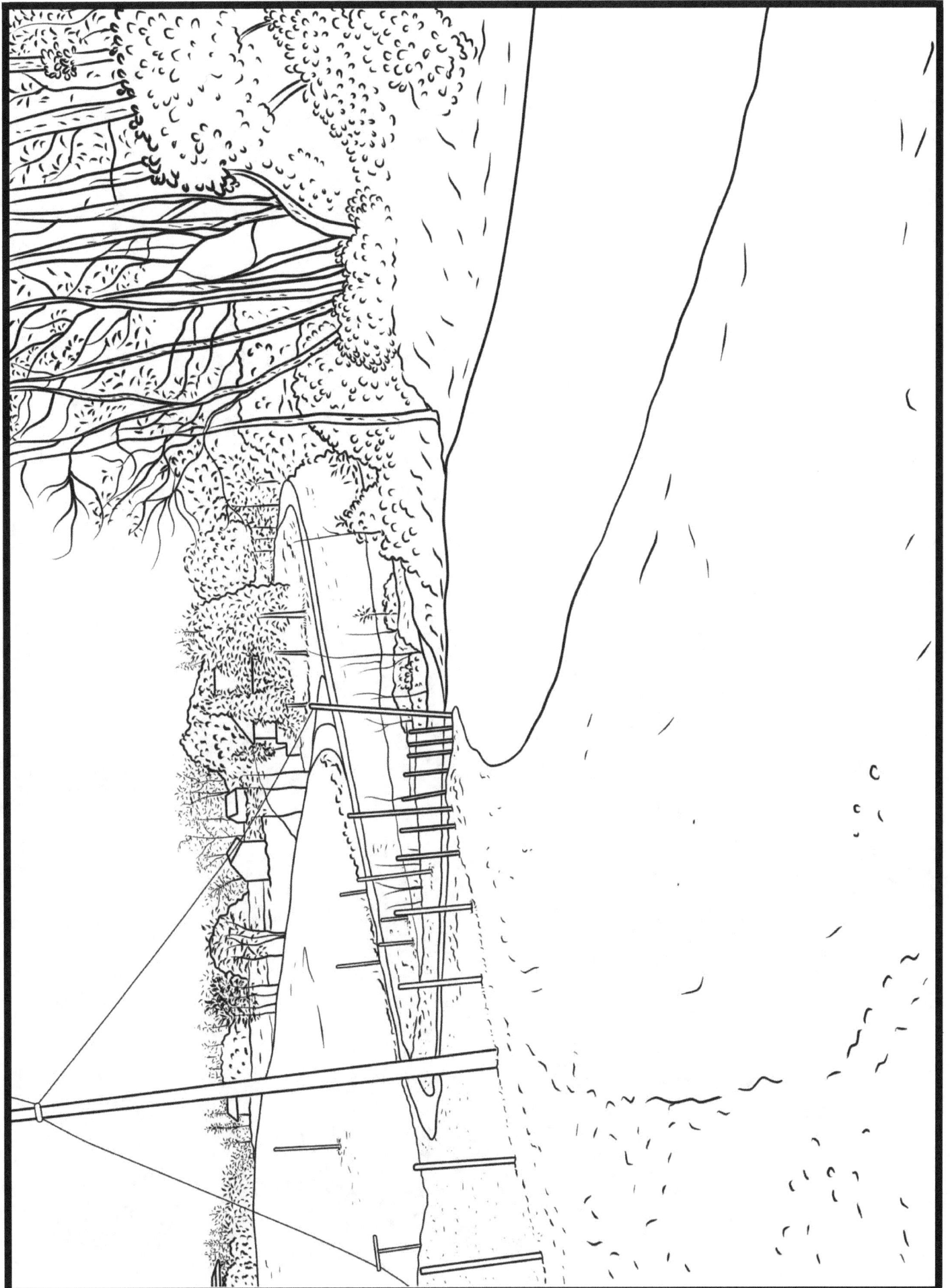

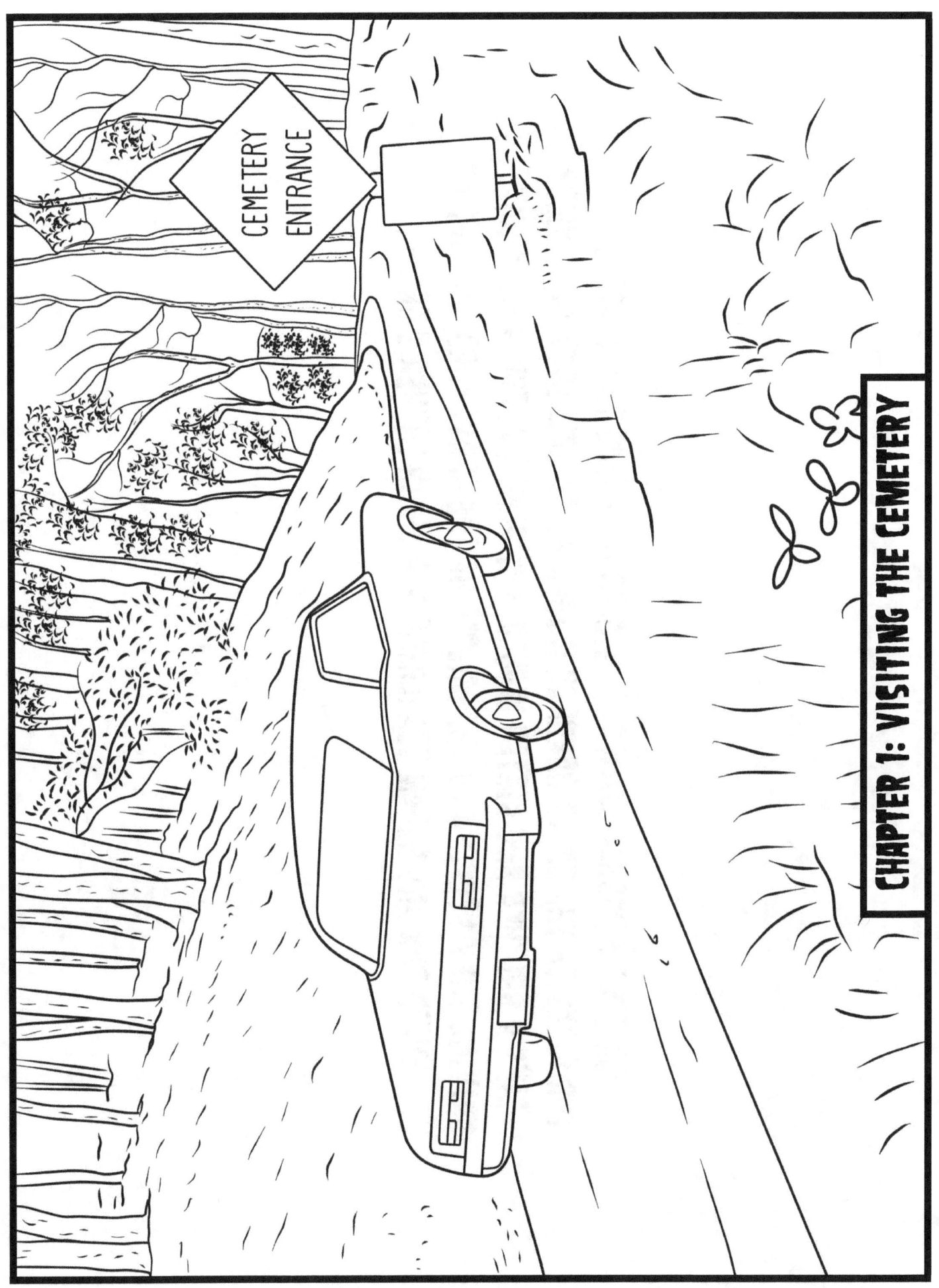

CEMETERY ENTRANCE

CHAPTER 1: VISITING THE CEMETERY

OUR STORY BEGINS WITH TWO SIBLINGS DRVING TO A CEMETERY.
FOR MOST OF THE DRIVE BARBARA & JOHNNY COMPLAINED AND FOUGHT
LIKE A BROTHER AND SISTER WOULD. BUT FINALLY, AFTER HOURS OF
DRIVING THEY STOPPED IN THE MIDDLE OF THE GRAVEYARD, GOT OUT OF
THEIR CAR AND BEGAN SEARCHING FOR THEIR FATHER'S GRAVE.

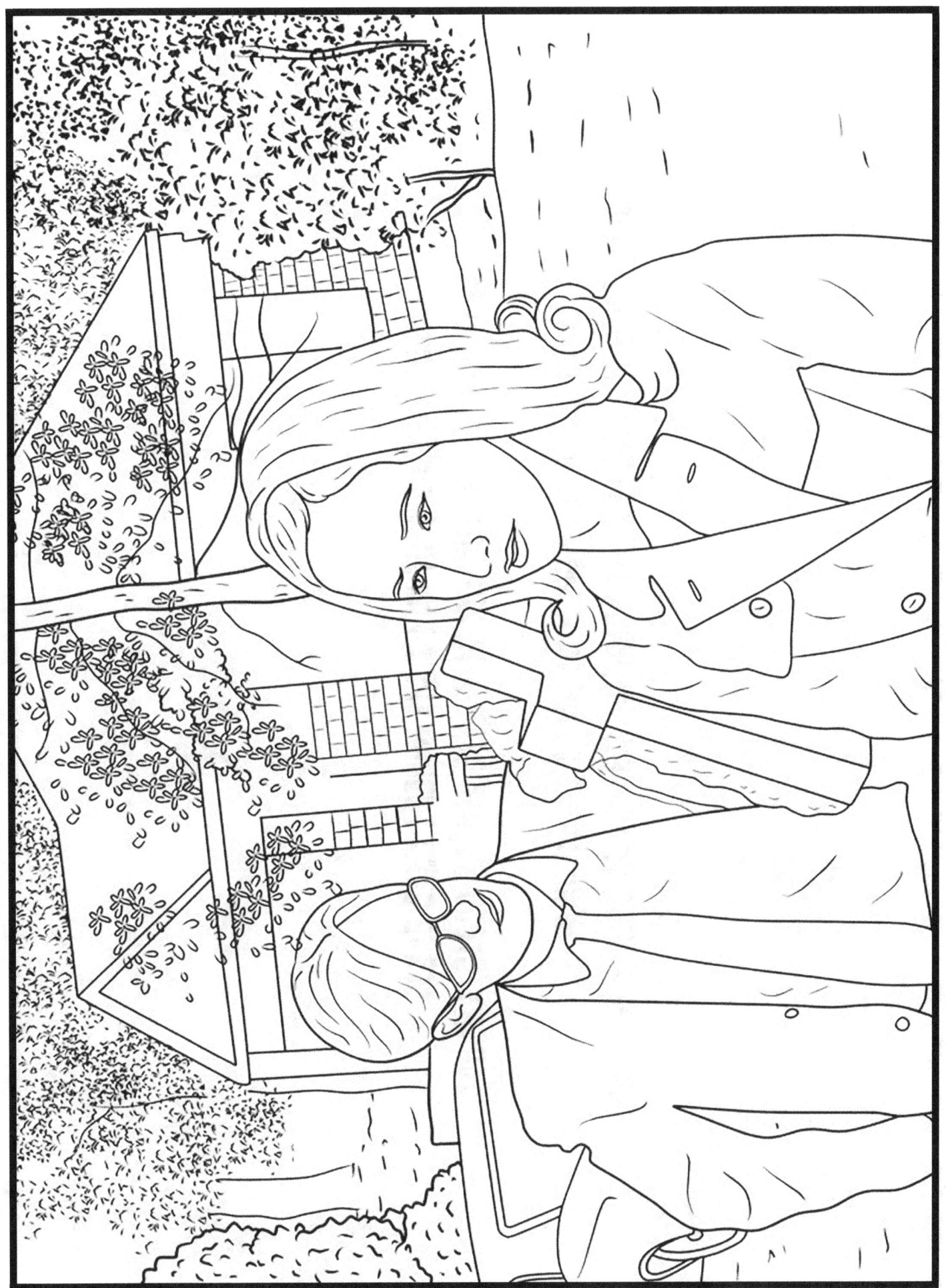

AFTER WALKING FOR A FEW MINUTES THEY FOUND THE GRAVESITE. BARBARA KNELT DOWN IN A MOMENT OF SILENCE.

JOHNNY STOOD BY HIS SISTER IMPATIENTLY. HE WAS READY TO LEAVE EVEN THOUGH THEY HAD JUST GOTTEN THERE.

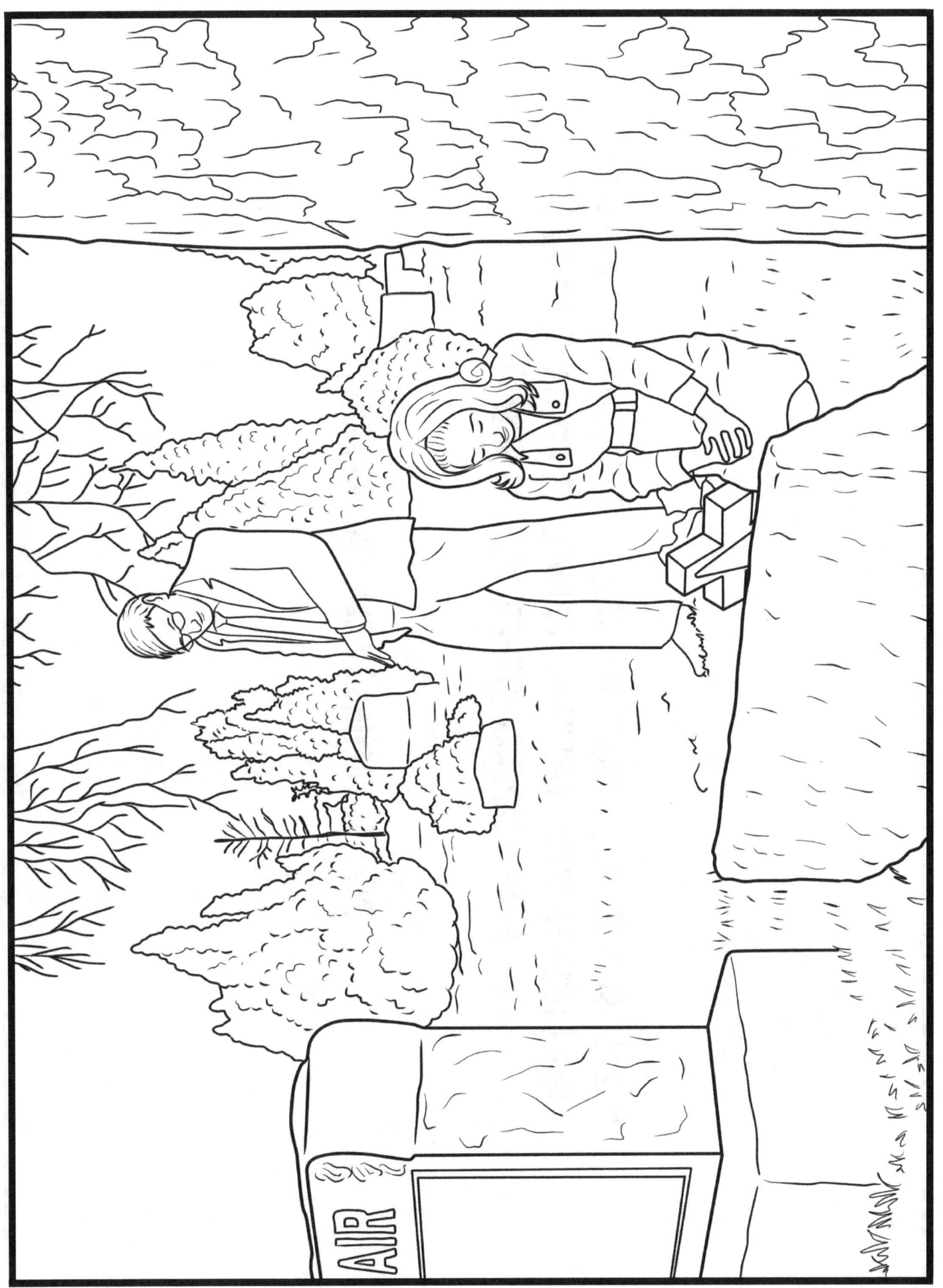

"HEY!" SAID JOHNNY, "DON'T YOU REMEMBER WHEN WE WERE KIDS AND I USED TO SCARE YOU HERE? YOU USED TO REALLY GET SCARED HERE." BARBARA STARTED FEELING UNEASY

"THEY'RE COMING TO GET YOU BARBARA!"

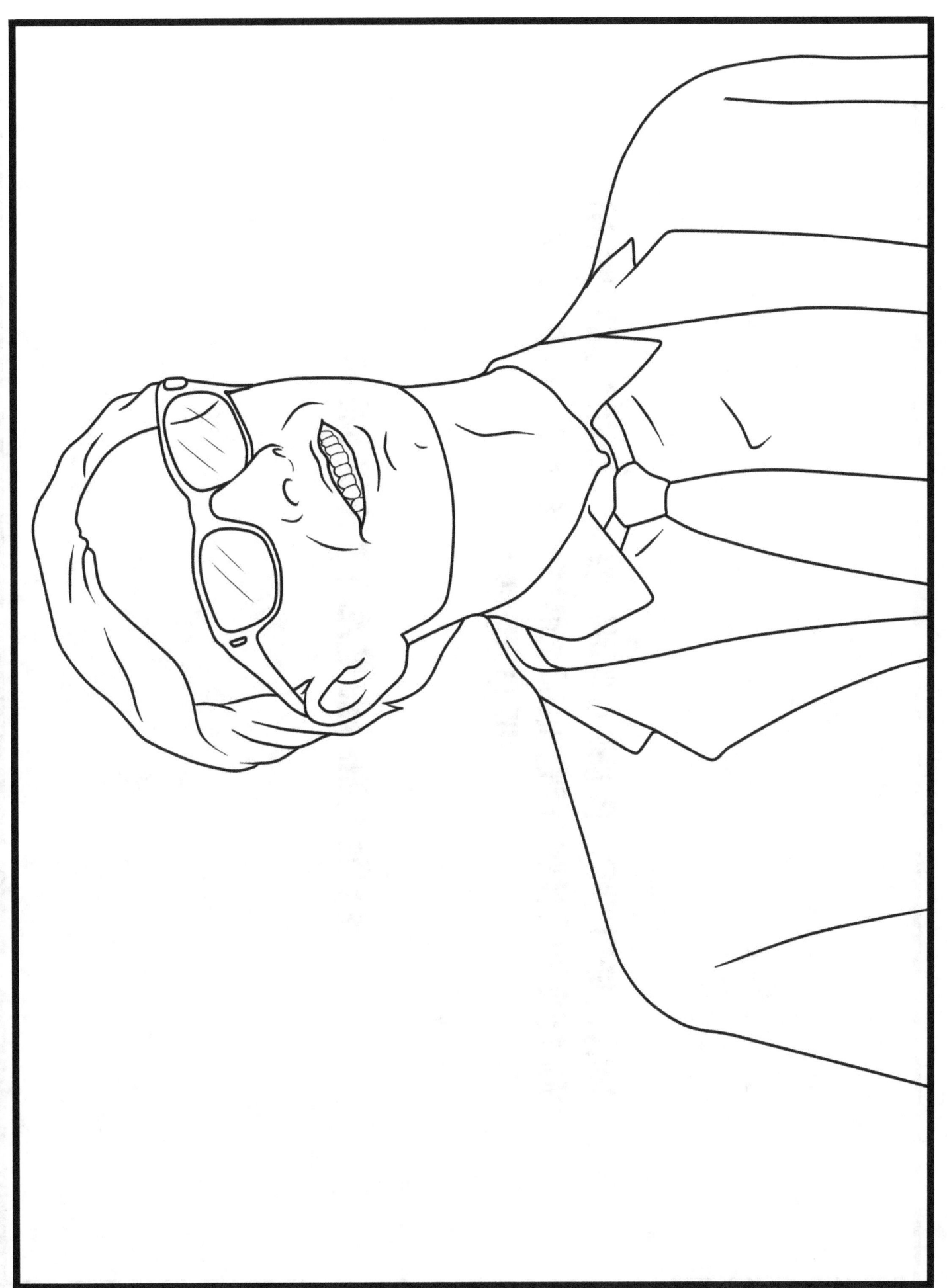

"WHY, LOOK! THERE IS ONE COMING FOR YOU NOW!" SAID JOHNNY POINTING TO A MAN WANDERING WANDERING ON THE OTHER SIDE OF THE CEMETERY

HE WAS ALONE AND APPEARED TO BE DRUNK

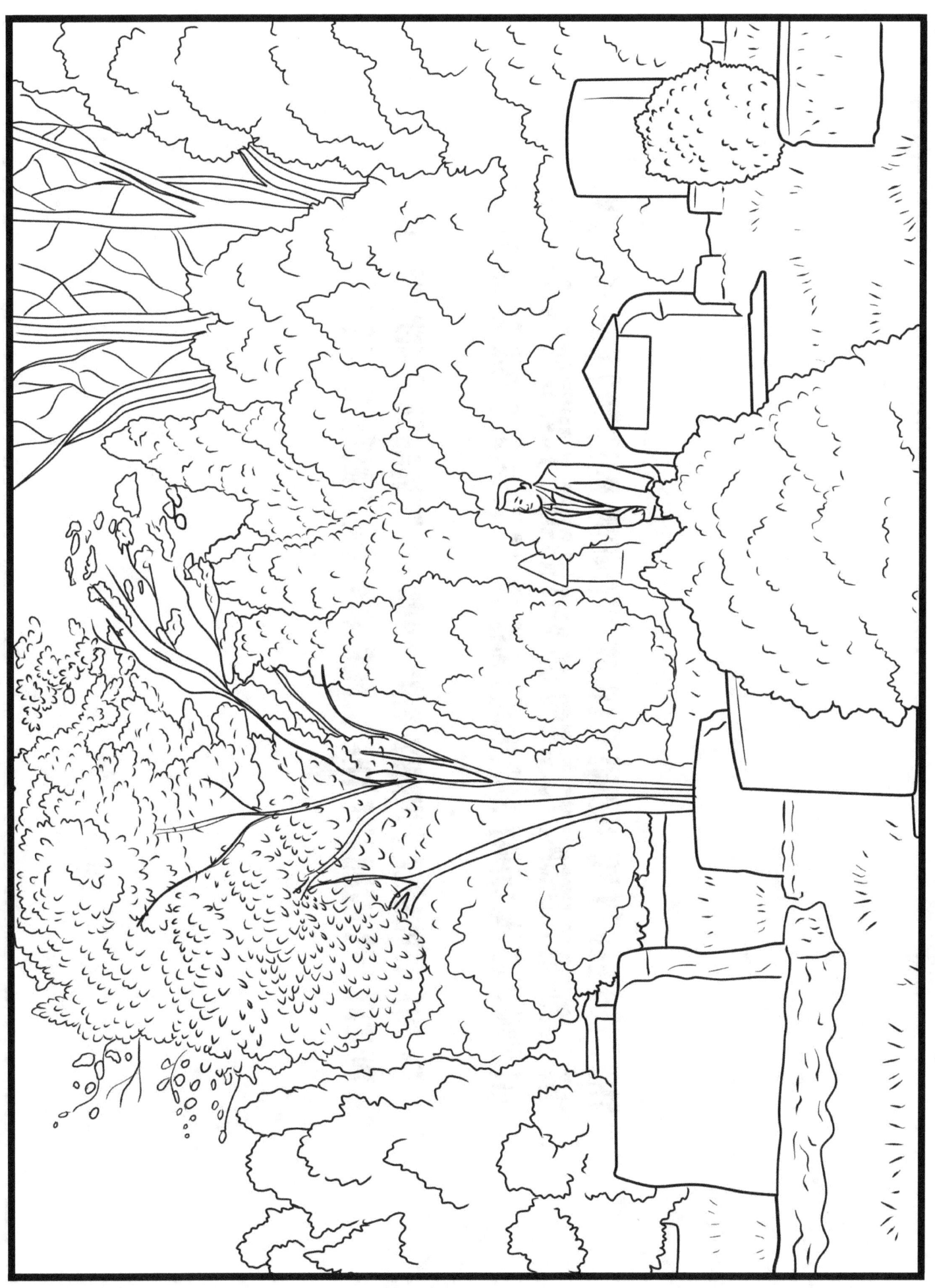

THE MAN BEGAN TO SLOWLY COME TOWARDS BARBARA AND JOHNNY.

HE SUDDENLY BEGAN TO SPEED UP AND RUSHED TOWARDS BARBARA!

JOHNNY SAW WHAT HAPPENED AND TRIED TO FIGHT THE MAN OFF.

IN THE STRUGGLE JOHNNY WAS THROWN TOWARDS A HEADSTONE

WHERE HIS HEAD HIT THE STONE AND WAS KNOCKED OUT COLD....

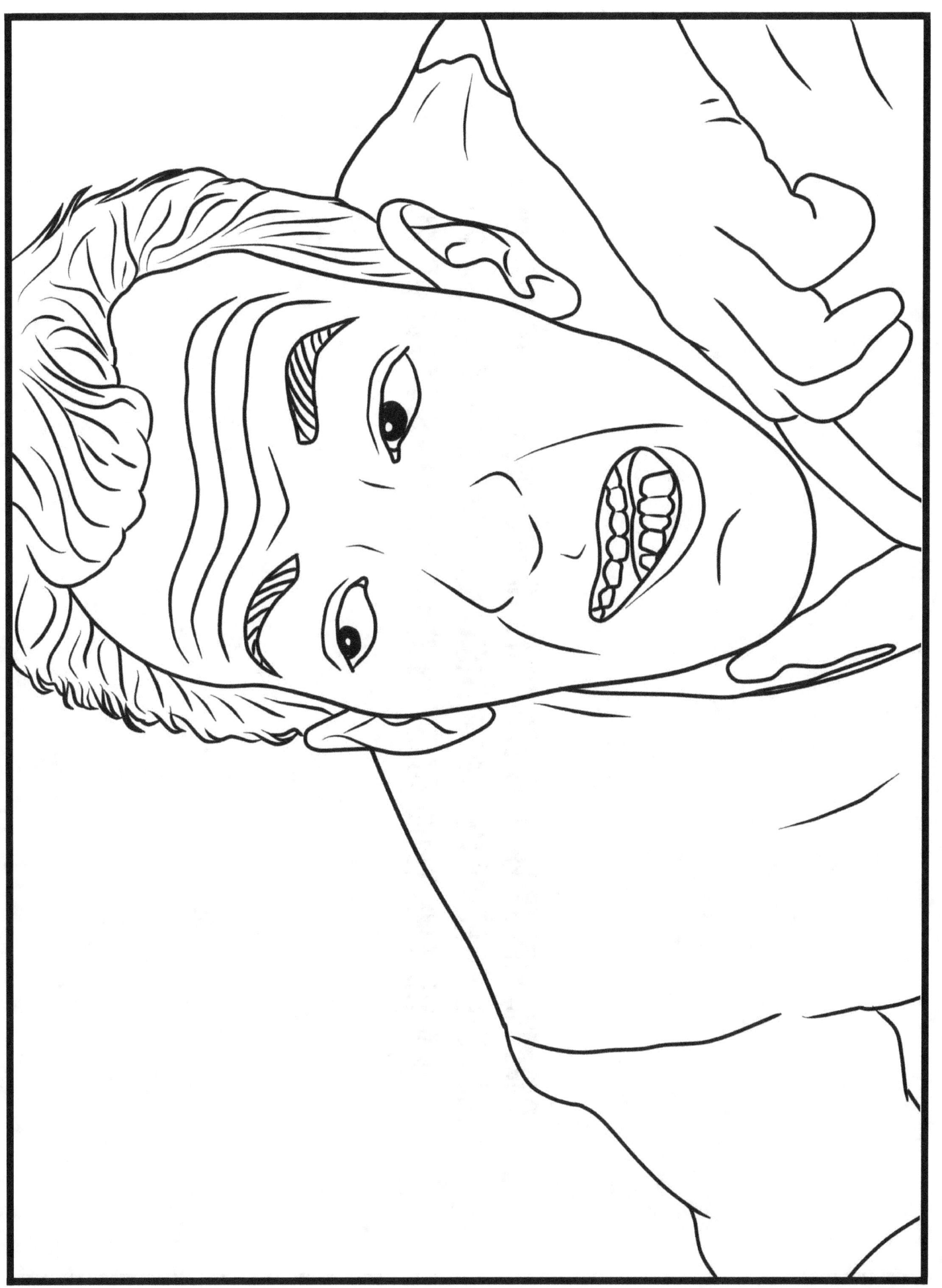

BARBARA RAN AS FAST AS SHE COULD TO THE CAR, ONLY TO FIND THAT THE KEYS WEREN'T IN THE IGNITION! SHE QUICKLY LOCKED THE DOORS AND THE MAN TRIED TO GET IN THE CAR IN ANYWAY POSSIBLE!

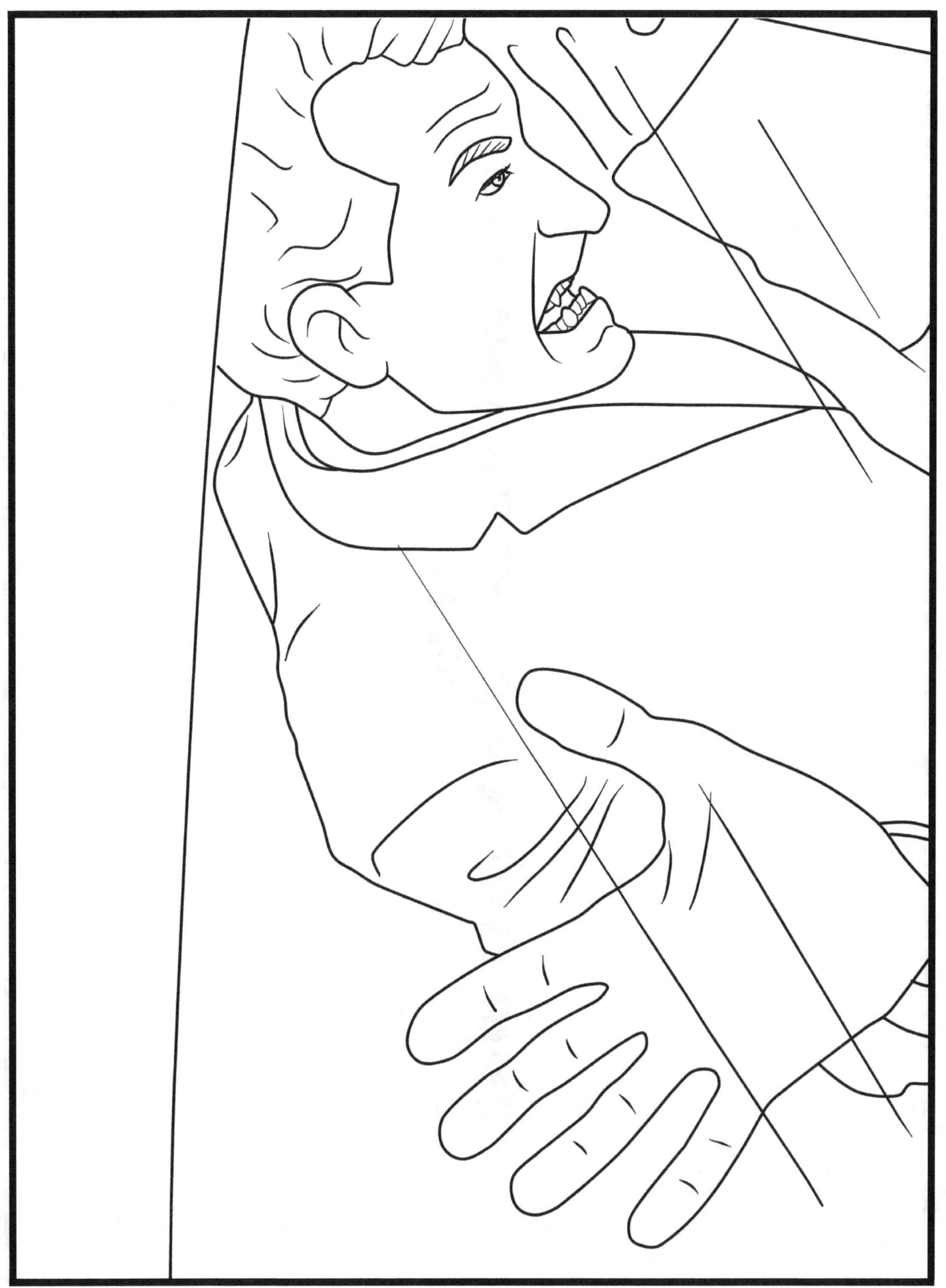

HE PICKED UP A ROCK AND BASHED AGAINST THE CAR WINDOW UNTIL IT SHATTERED!

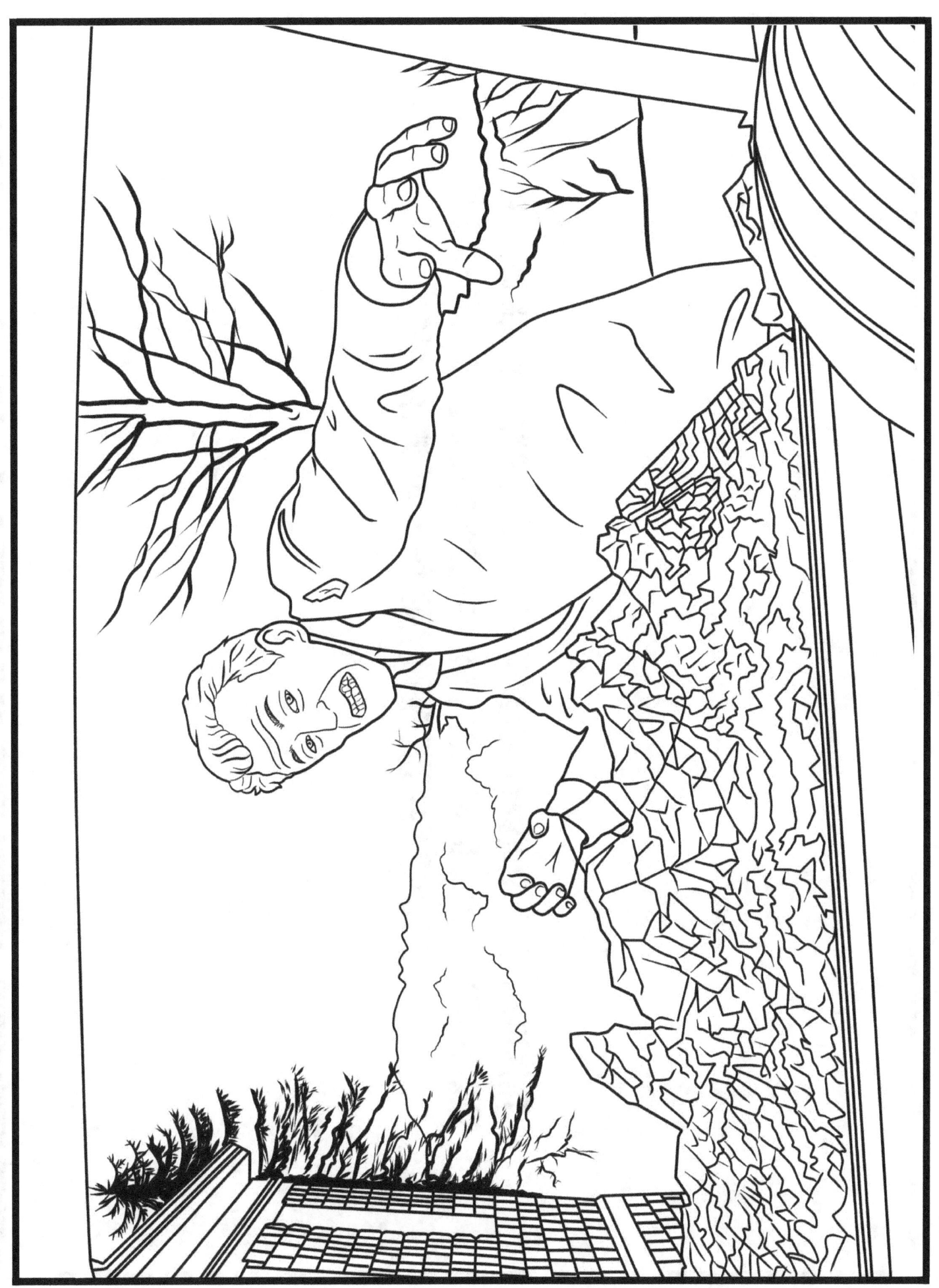

THINKING FAST, BARBARA RELEASED THE EMERGENCY BREAK AND THE CAR BEGAN TO ROLL DOWN THE ROAD! BARBARA LOOKED IN THE MIRROR AND COULD SEE THE MAN WAS CHASING AFTER HER!

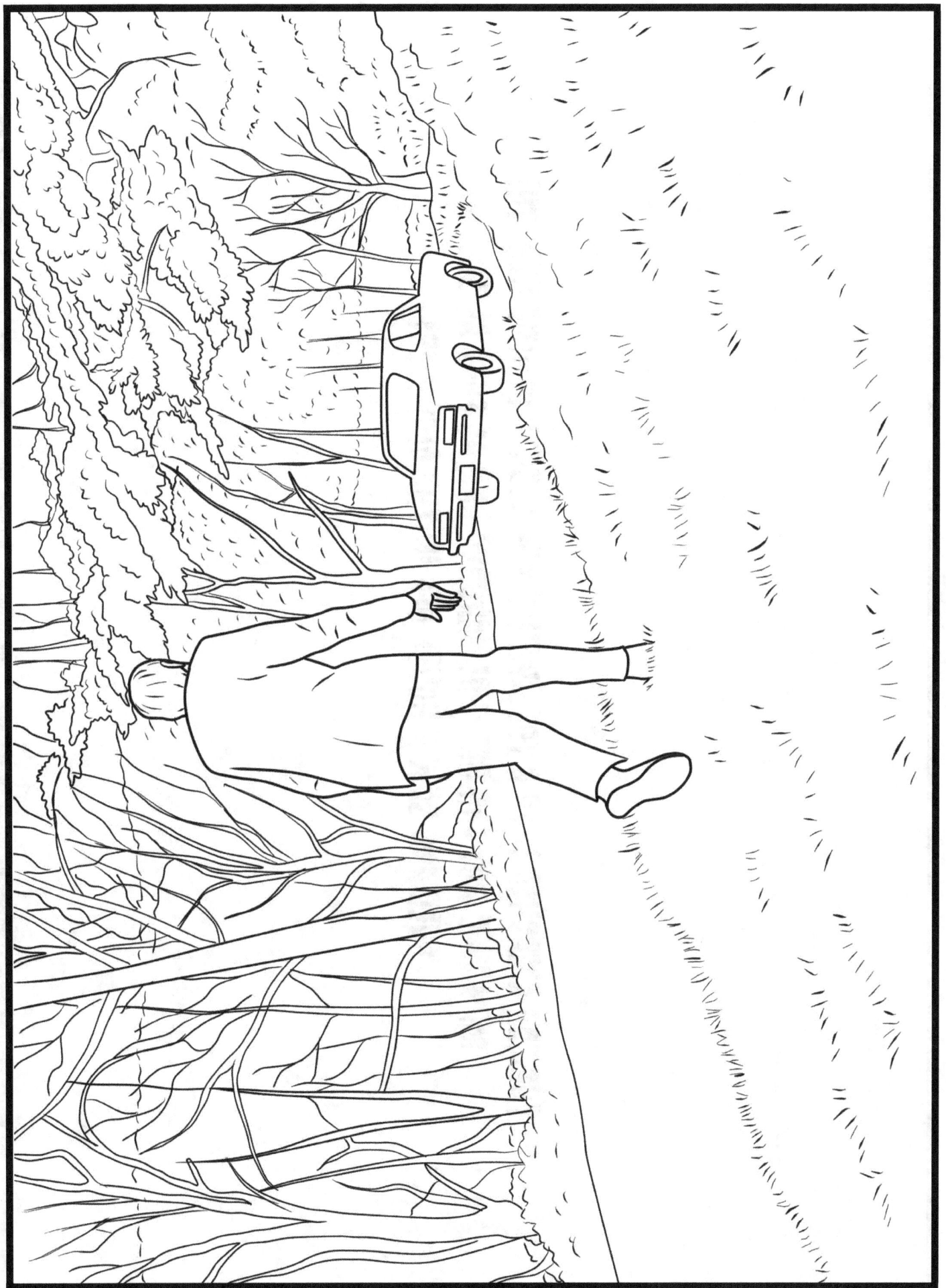

THE CAR SMASHED INTO A TREE WHILE SHE LOOKED BEHIND HER. THE MAN WAS NOT FAR BEHIND! BARBARA RAN AS FAST AS SHE COULD AND SAW A HOUSE OFF IN THE DISTANCE!

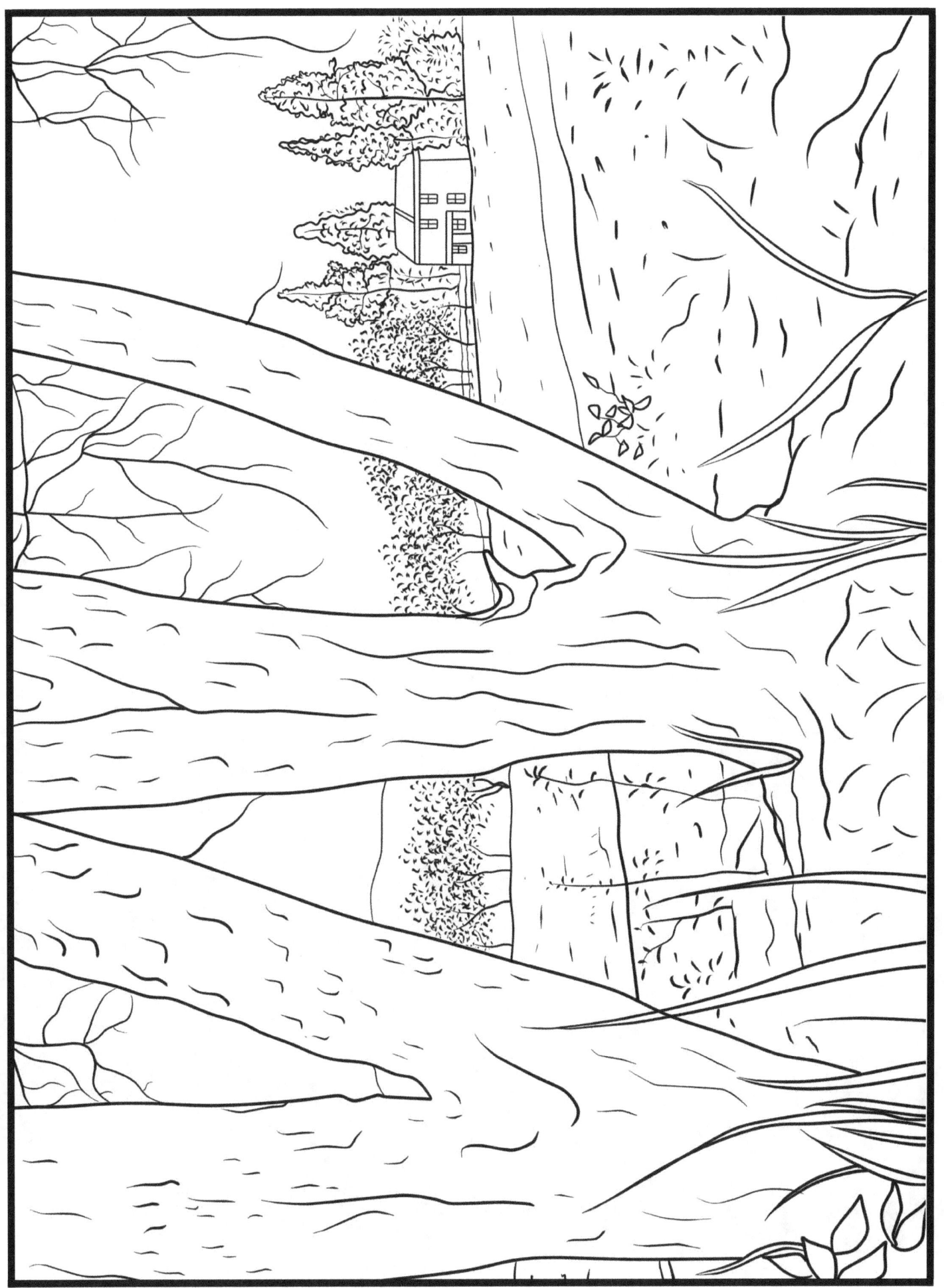

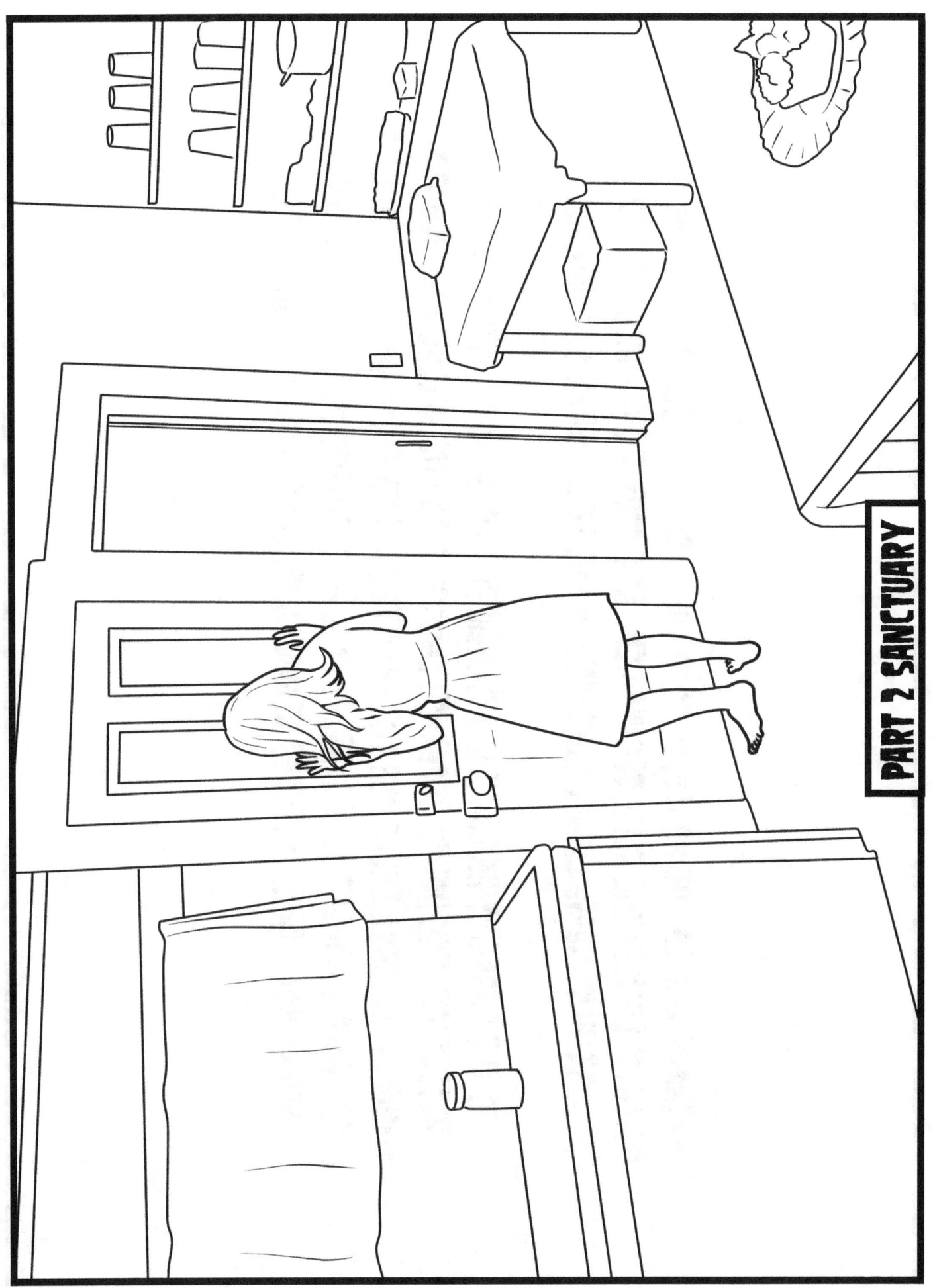

PART 2 SANCTUARY

BARBARA RAN TO THE HOUSE, OPENED THE BACK DOOR, JUMPED INSIDE, AND QUICKLY LOCKED THE DOOR BEHIND HER! SHE TOOK A DEEP BREATH, STARTED GAINING SOME COMPOSURE, AND BEGAN TO EXPLORE THE HOUSE.

AS SHE PASSED THROUGH THE KITCHEN SHE GRABBED A CHEF KNIFE FOR PROTECTION. THE HOUSE APPEARED EMPTY & AS SHE PEERED THROUGH THE WINDOW BARBARA COULD SEE THE MAN TRYING TO MAKE HIS WAY INSIDE! THERE WAS NOWHERE TO GET HELP! IT WAS STARTING TO GET DARK OUTSIDE, AND SLOWLY MORE FIGURES BEGAN TO EMERGE FROM THE DARKNESS...

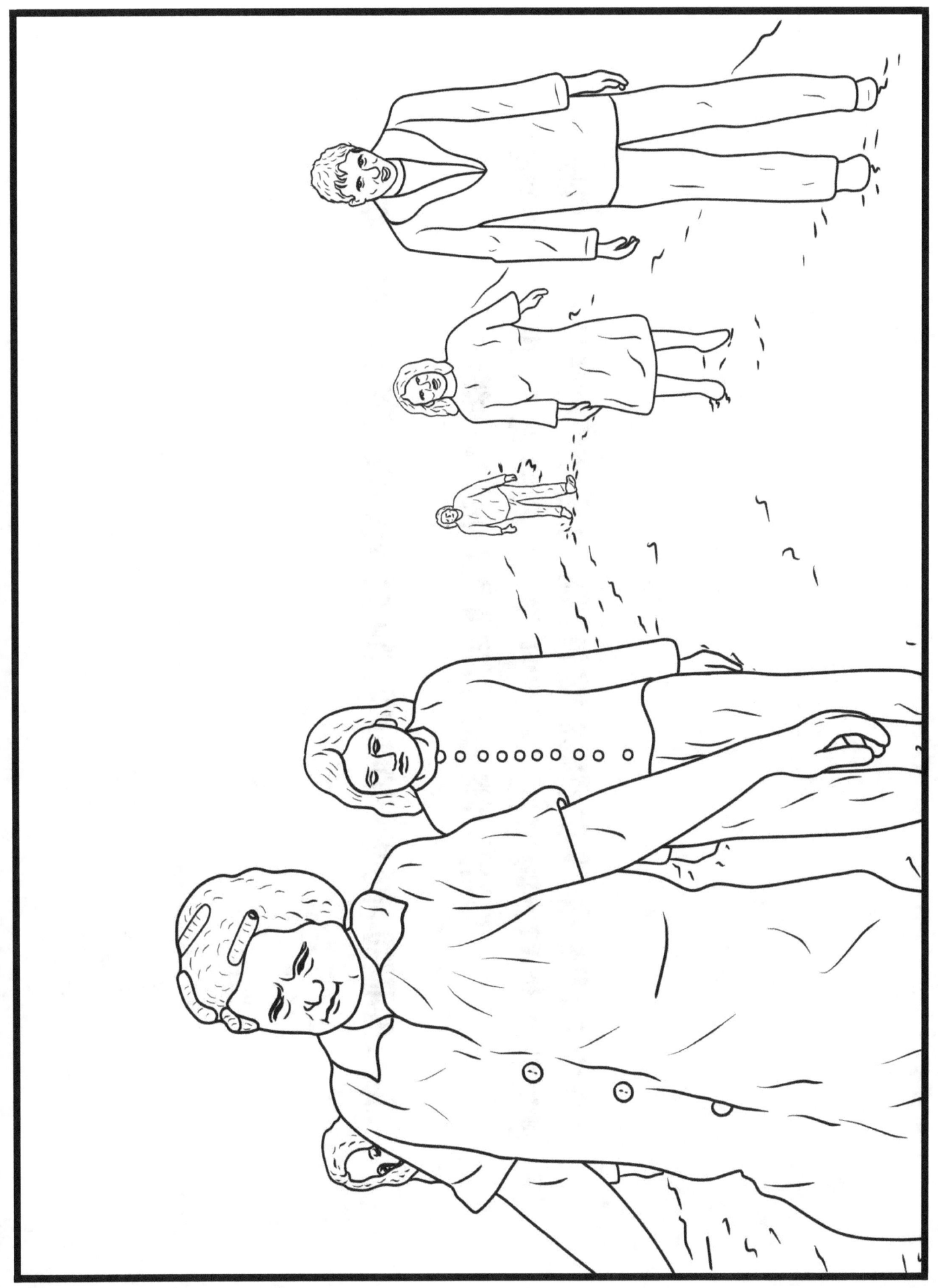

AFTER SEEING THESE THESE STRANGE PEOPLE OUTSIDE, BARBARA QUICKLY RAN UPSTAIRS TO TRY AND FIND SAFETY! TO HER HORROR, AT THE TOP OF THE STAIRS SHE RAN INTO A ROTTING CORPSE!

SHE SCREAMED AND RUSHED DOWNSTAIRS AND THROUGH THE FONT DOOR!

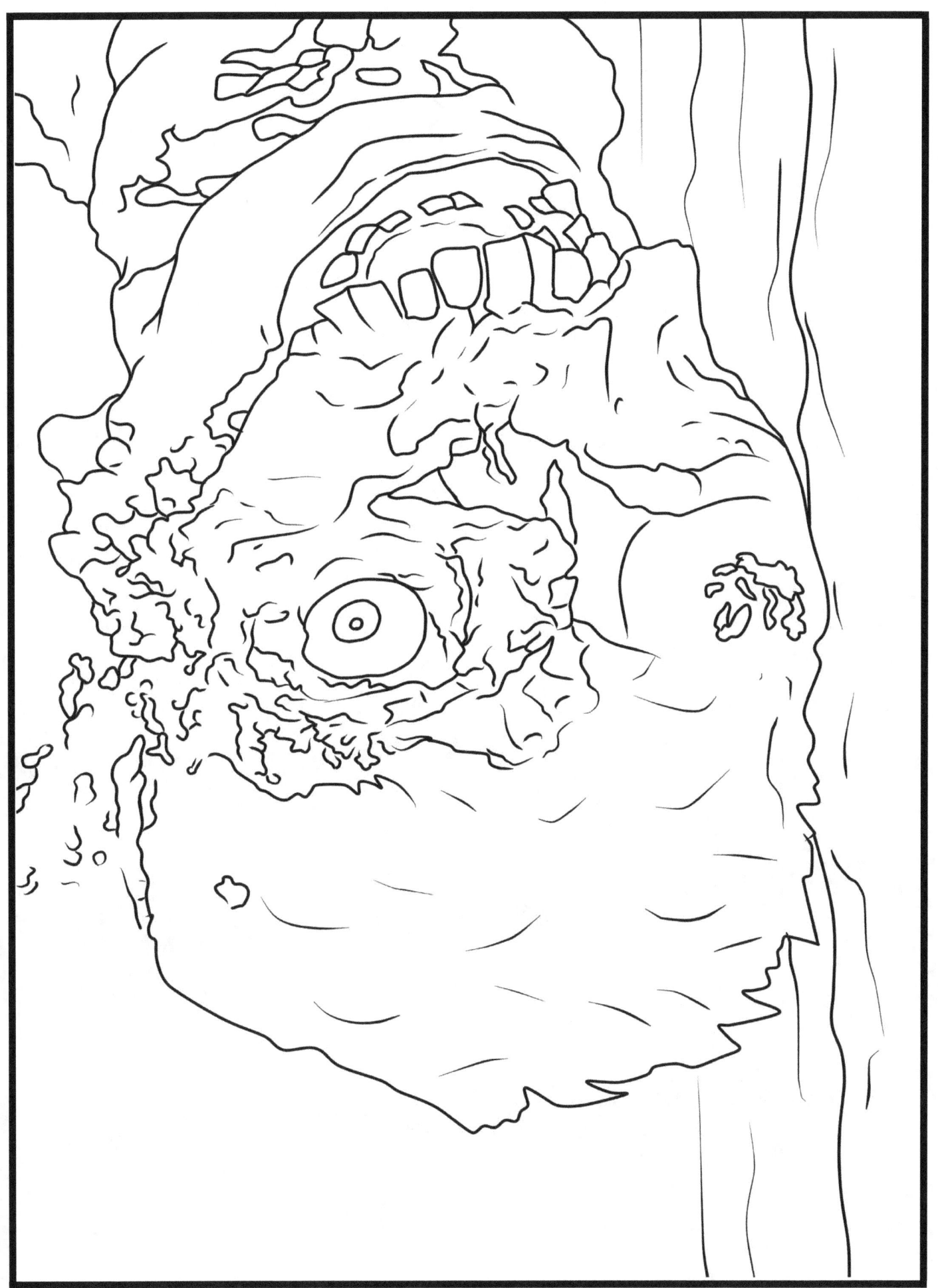

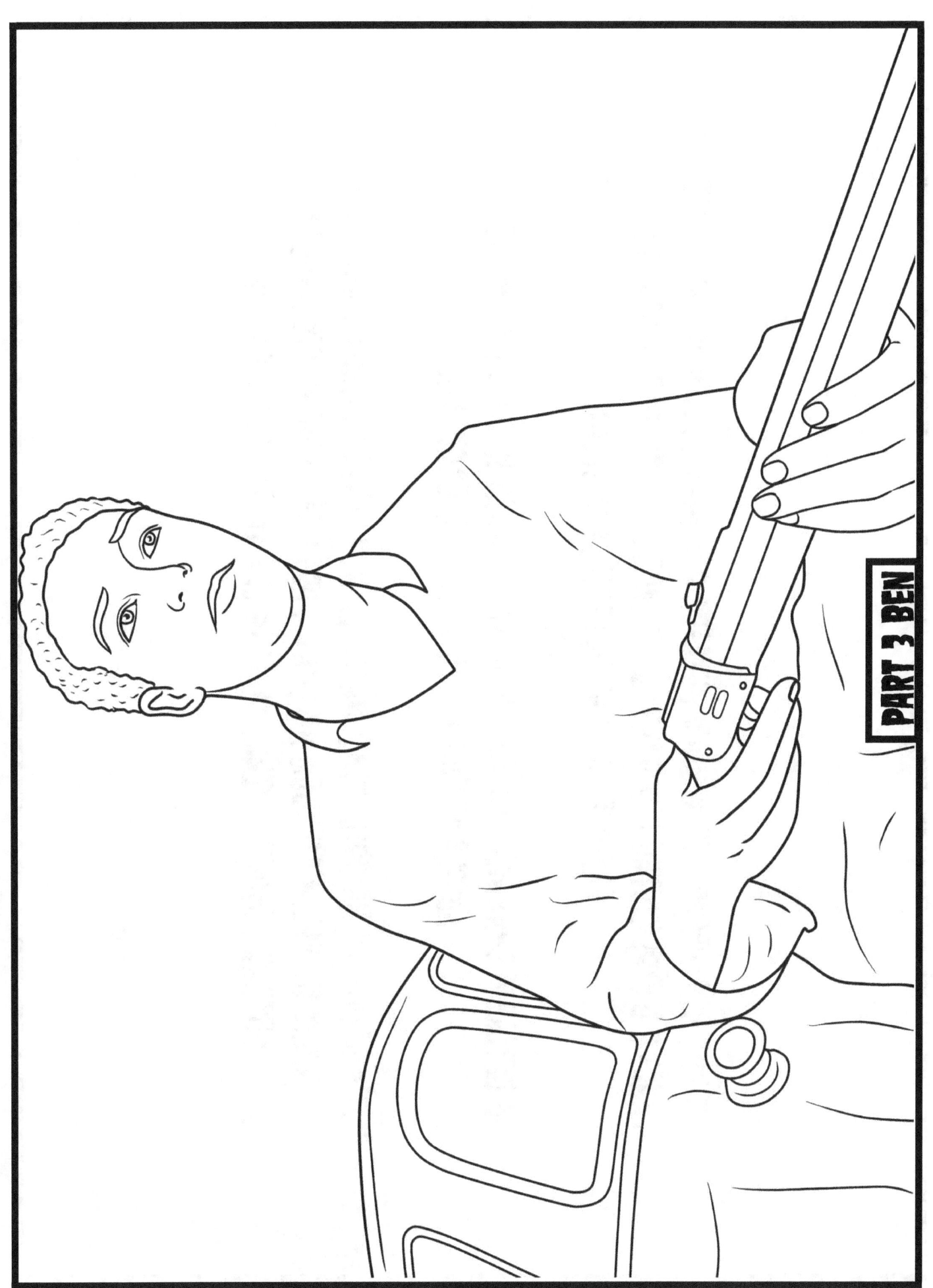

PART 3 BEN

AS SHE SCREAMED AND RUSHED OUTSIDE BARBARA WAS STOPPED IN HER TRACKS BY BLINDING HEADLIGHTS. IT WAS A TRUCK AND FROM THE CAB EMERGED A MAN HOLDING A SHOTGUN.

HE QUICKLY GRABBED HER AND TOOK THEM BOTH INSIDE. HE BOLTED THE DOOR AND TURNED TO SPEAK TO BARBARA.

"IT'S ALRIGHT" HE SAID, "MY NAME IS BEN. THERE WILL PROBABLY BE MORE OF THEM AS SOON AS THEY FIND US! DO YOU LIVE HERE?" BARBARA DIDN'T SPEAK. "WE'VE GOT TO GET OUT OF HERE!"

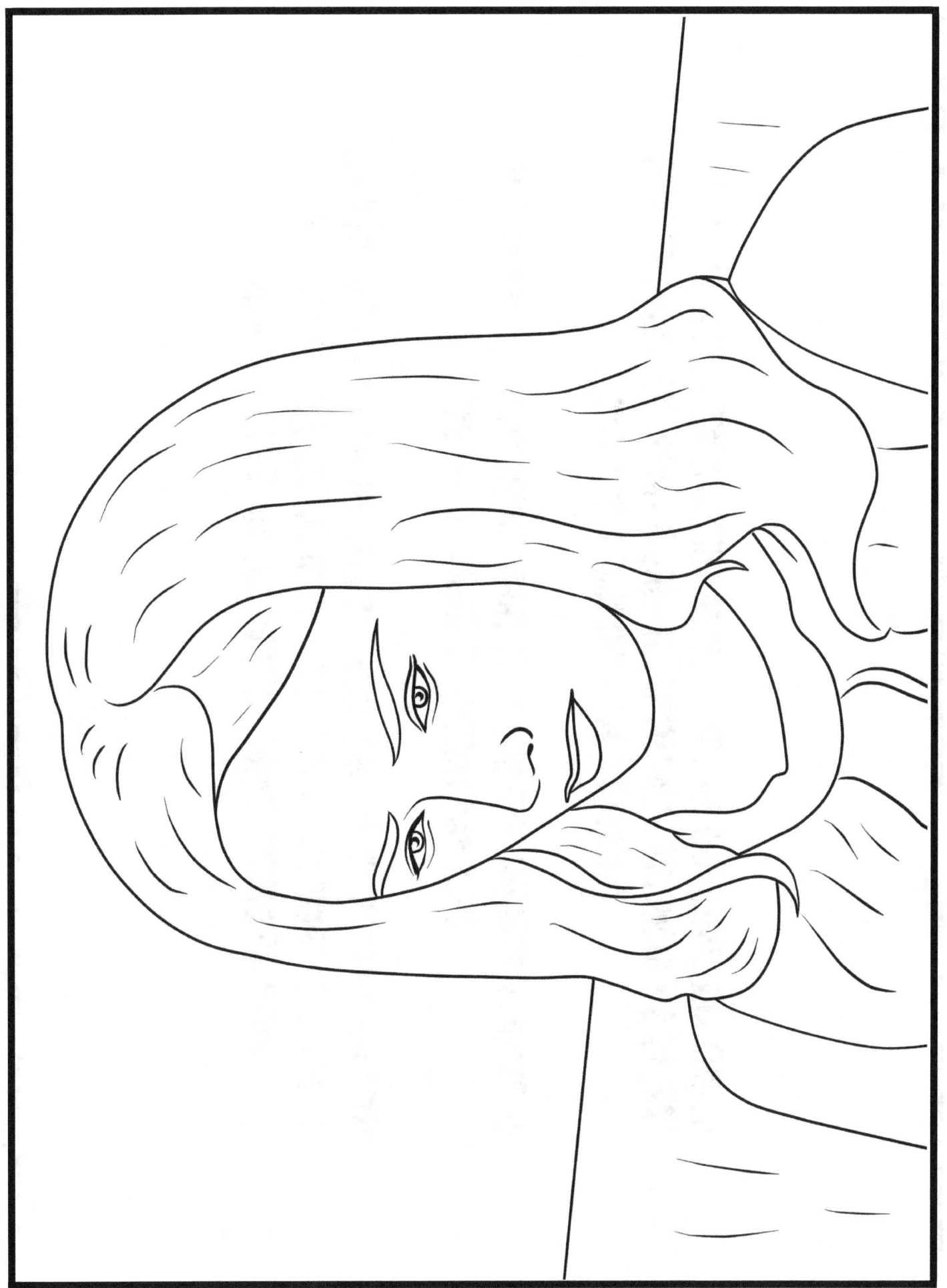

AS SHE SCREAMED AND RUSHED OUTSIDE BARBARA WAS STOPPED IN HER TRACKS BY BLINDING HEADLIGHTS. IT WAS A TRUCK AND FROM THE CAB EMERGED A MAN HOLDING A SHOTGUN.

HE QUICKLY GRABBED HER AND TOOK THEM BOTH INSIDE. HE BOLTED THE DOOR AND TURNED TO SPEAK TO BARBARA.

"IT'S ALRIGHT" HE SAID, "MY NAME IS BEN. THERE WILL PROBABLY BE MORE OF THEM AS SOON AS THEY FIND US! DO YOU LIVE HERE?" BARBARA DIDN'T SPEAK. "WE'VE GOT TO GET OUT OF HERE!"

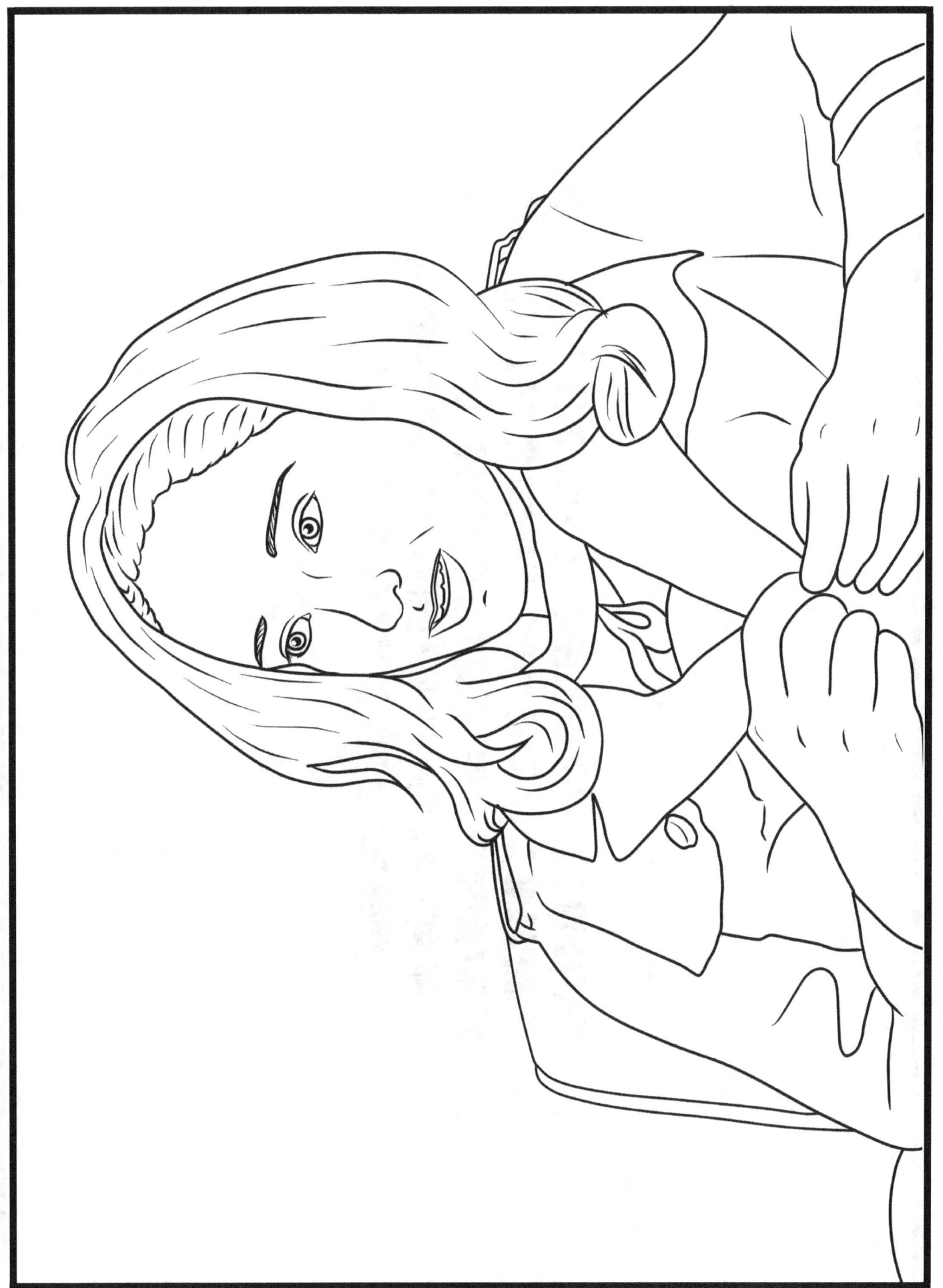

SHE STARTED TO FALL INTO HYSTERICS! SAYING THEY HAD TO GO AND GET JOHNNY AND SAVE HIM! "YOUR BROTHER IS DEAD!" BEN SAID. BARBARA INSISTED THAT HE WASN'T ATTACKED BEN. BARBARA SLAPPED HIM IN THE FACE AND BEN HIT HER BACK! SHE THEN PASSED OUT. BEN THEN PLACED HER ON THE COUCH TO RECOVER.

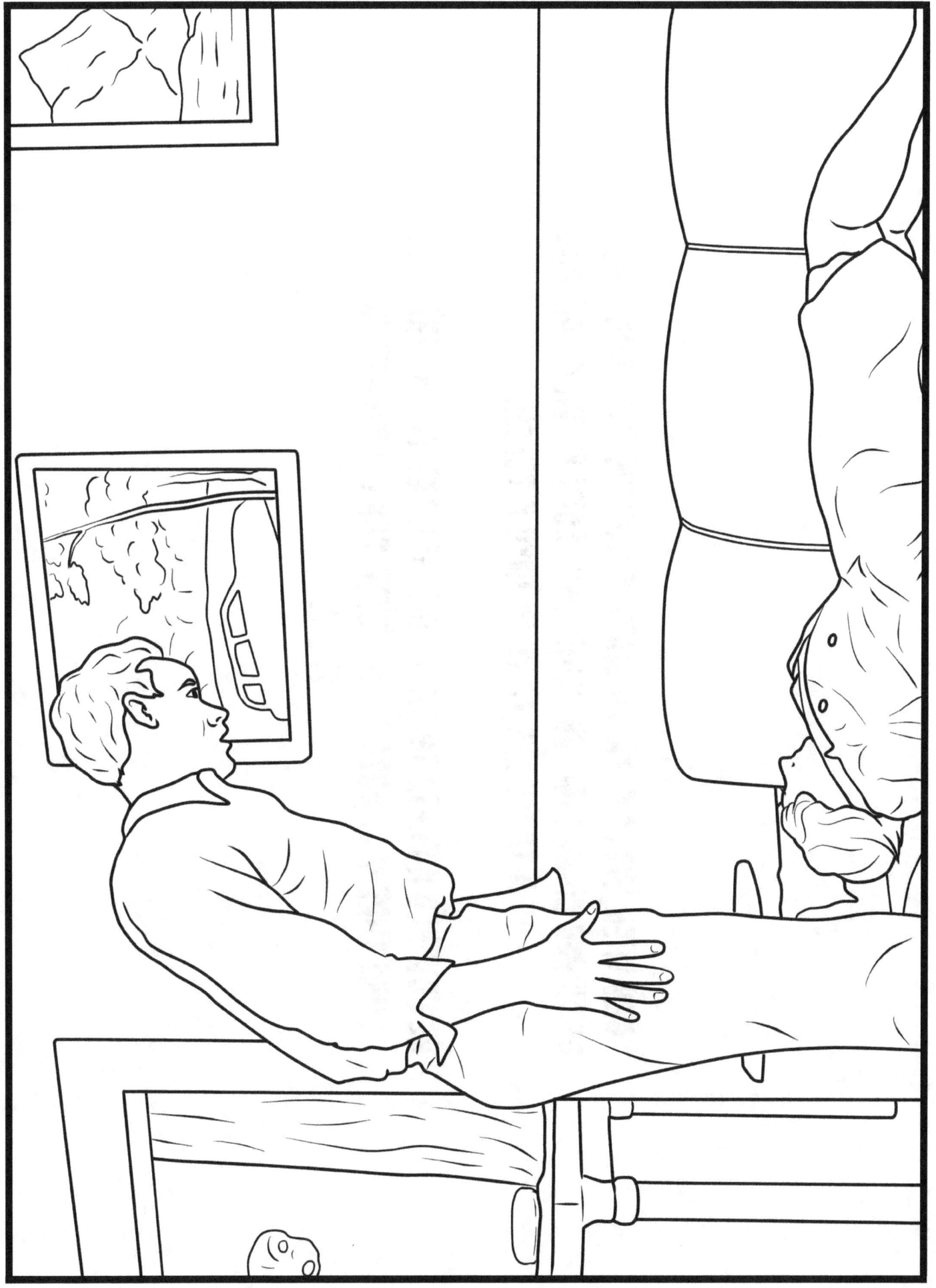

BEN THEN WENT BACK TO WORK SECURING THE HOUSE. HE GATHERED SOME LIGHTER FLUID AND CLOTH TO WRAP AROUND A TABLE LEG TO TURN INTO A TORCH.

HE COVERED A CHAIR IN LIGHTER FLUID, SET IT ON FIRE, AND THEN THREW IT OUTSIDE TO DETER THE CREATURES FROM THEM.

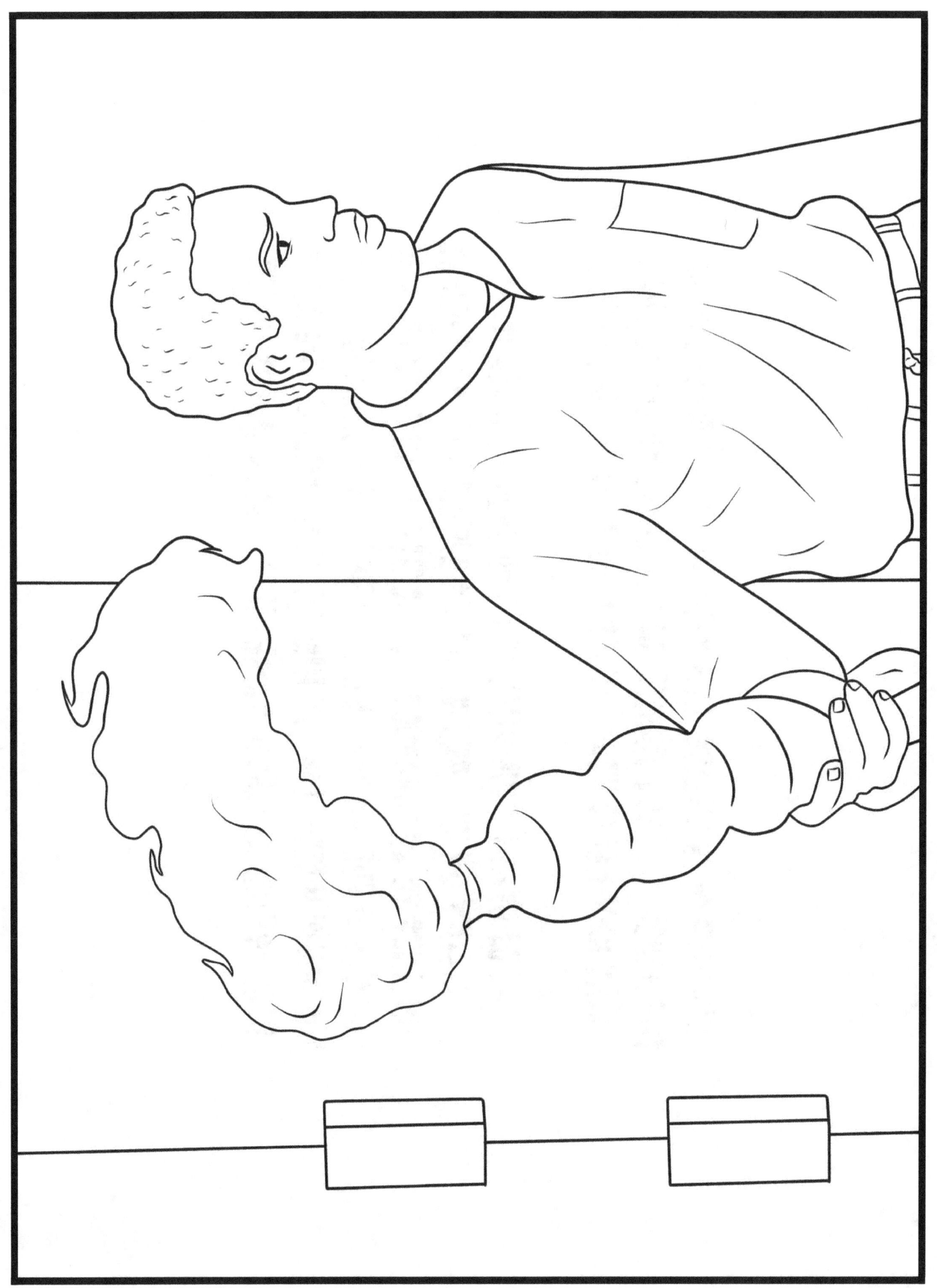

RUSHING BACK INSIDE, BEN KEPT WORKING ON SECURING THE HOUSE. HE ALSO TURNED ON THE RADIO TO SEE IF THERE WAS ANY NEWS ABOUT WHAT WAS EXACTLY GOING ON.

THE DJ BEGAN, "WE WILL NOT END THIS BROADCAST, IT WILL STAY ON DAY AND NIGHT. AS EMERGENCY PERSONNEL CONTINUE TO BE MBARDED WITH CALLS..STAY INDOORS AND DO NOT LEAVE YOUR HOMES...." BEN THEN STARTED TAK-ING DOWN A DOOR OFF ITS HINGES TO BARRICADE THE MAIN DOOR WHICH REVEALED SOMETHING HIDDEN IN THE HOUSE

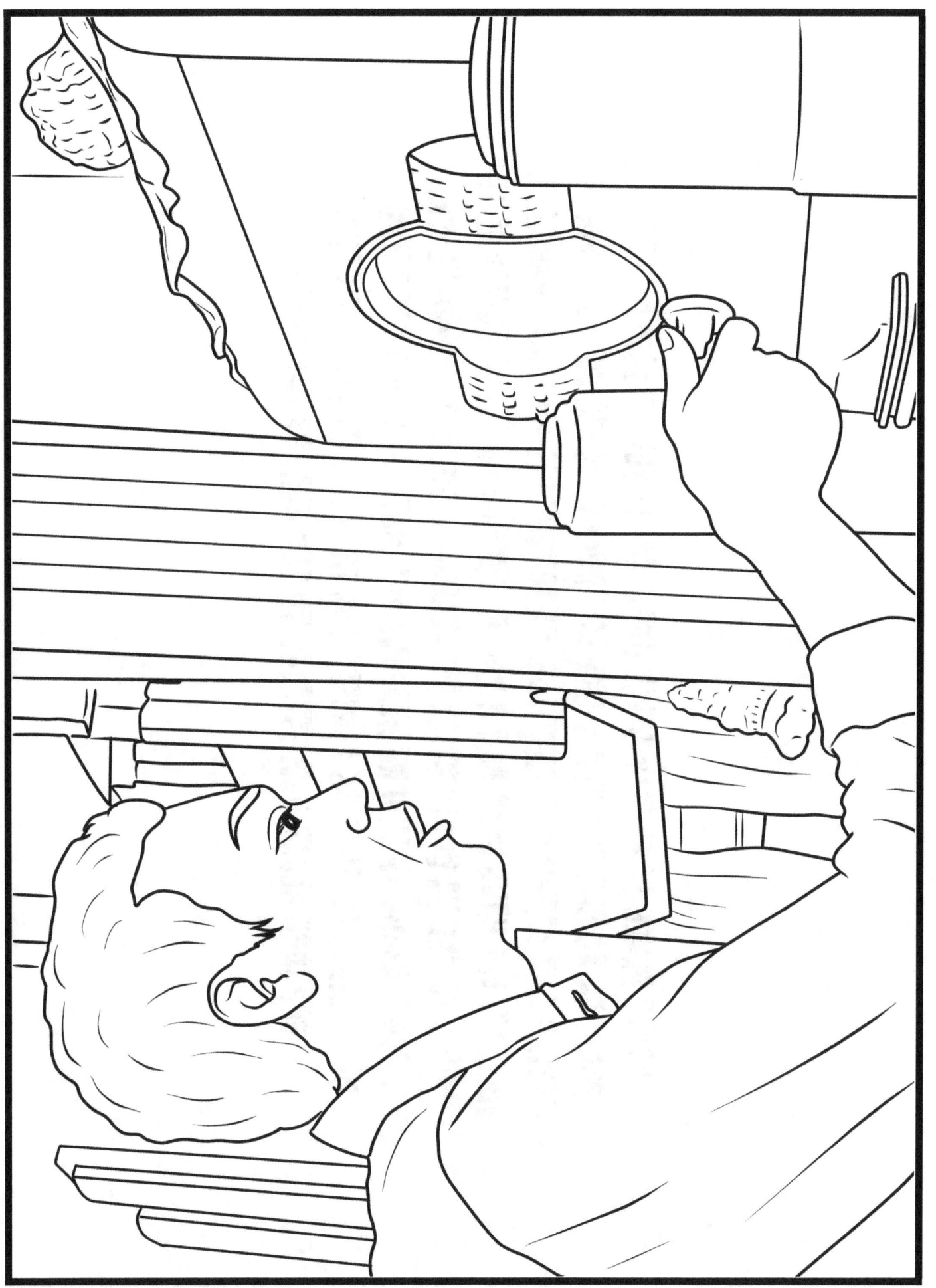

"THIS PLACE IS PRETTY WELL BOARDED UP NOW," SAID BEN TO BARBARA AS SHE SLOWLY WOKE UP FROM PASSING OUT. SHE WAS SITTING AND STARING AT NOTHING. "I FOUND THIS GUN OUT THERE AND BULLETS, WE HAVE FOOD AND A RADIO. SOONER OR LATER SOMEONE IS BOUND TO GET US OUT!" STILL NO RESPONSE FROM BARBARA "LOOK, I DON'T KNOW IF YOU'RE HEARING ME, BUT I'M GOING UPSTAIRS NOW......EVERYTHING IS ALRIGHT FOR NOW.." AND BEN THEN LEFT BARBARA ALONE DOWNSTAIRS TO THE HUM OF THE RADIO.

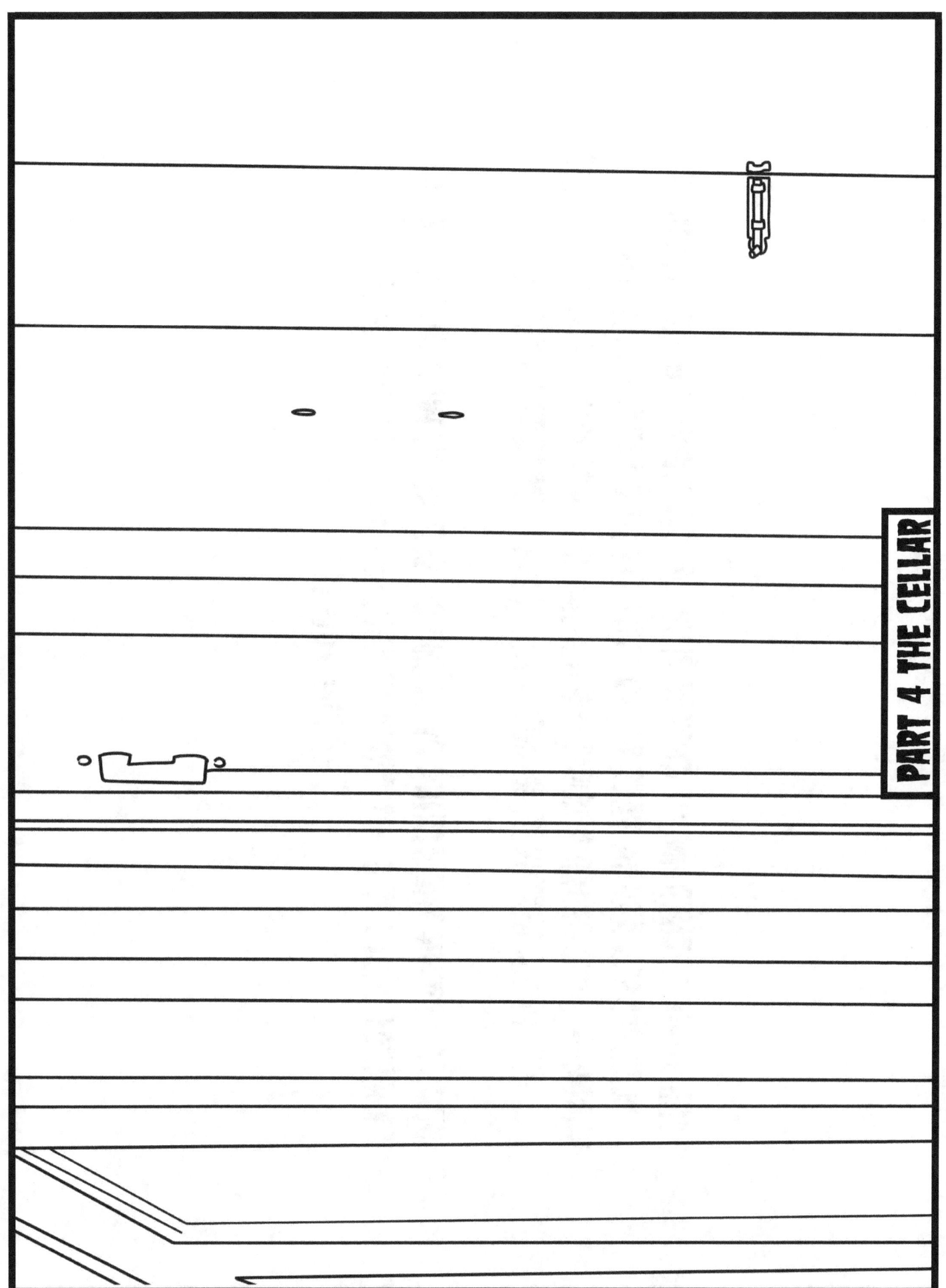

PART 4 THE CELLAR

THE RADIO DRONED ON, "I REPEAT THIS LATEST NEWS BULLETIN, THESE MURDERERS ARE IN FACT EATING THE FLESH OF THEIR VICTIMS..." BARBARA THEN HEARD A RUSTLING BEHIND HER AND OUT JUMPED 2 MEN! ONE HAD A MACHETE, READY FOR A FIGHT! BARBARA SCREAMED!

BEN RAN DOWN THE STAIRS AT SOUND OF SCREAMS, WITH HIS SHOTGUN IN HAND! "HOLD IT DON'T SHOOT!" SAID ONE OF THE TWO MEN! "WE'RE FROM TOWN!"

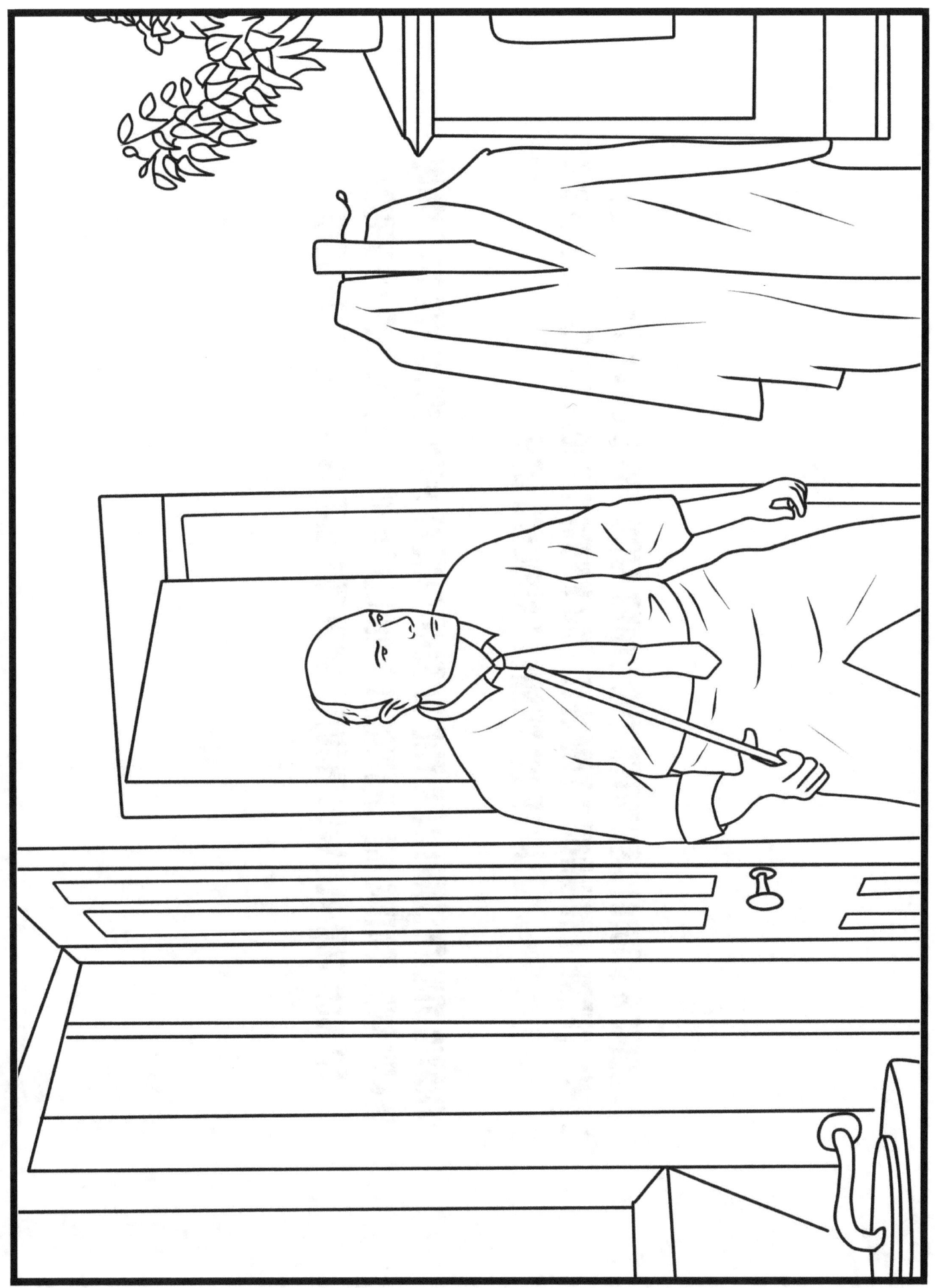

"LOOK A RADIO!" SHOUTED THE OTHER MAN "YOU GUYS HAVE BEEN DOWN THERE THE WHOLE TIME?!? YOU KNOW I COULD HAVE USED SOME HELP UP THERE!" SHOUTED BEN

"THAT'S THE CELLAR! IT'S THE SAFEST PLACE! HOW WERE WE TO KNOW WHAT WAS GOING ON UP HERE?! YOU COULD HAVE BEEN ONE OF THOSE THINGS FOR ALL WE KNEW!" SAID THE ONE WITH THE MACHETE

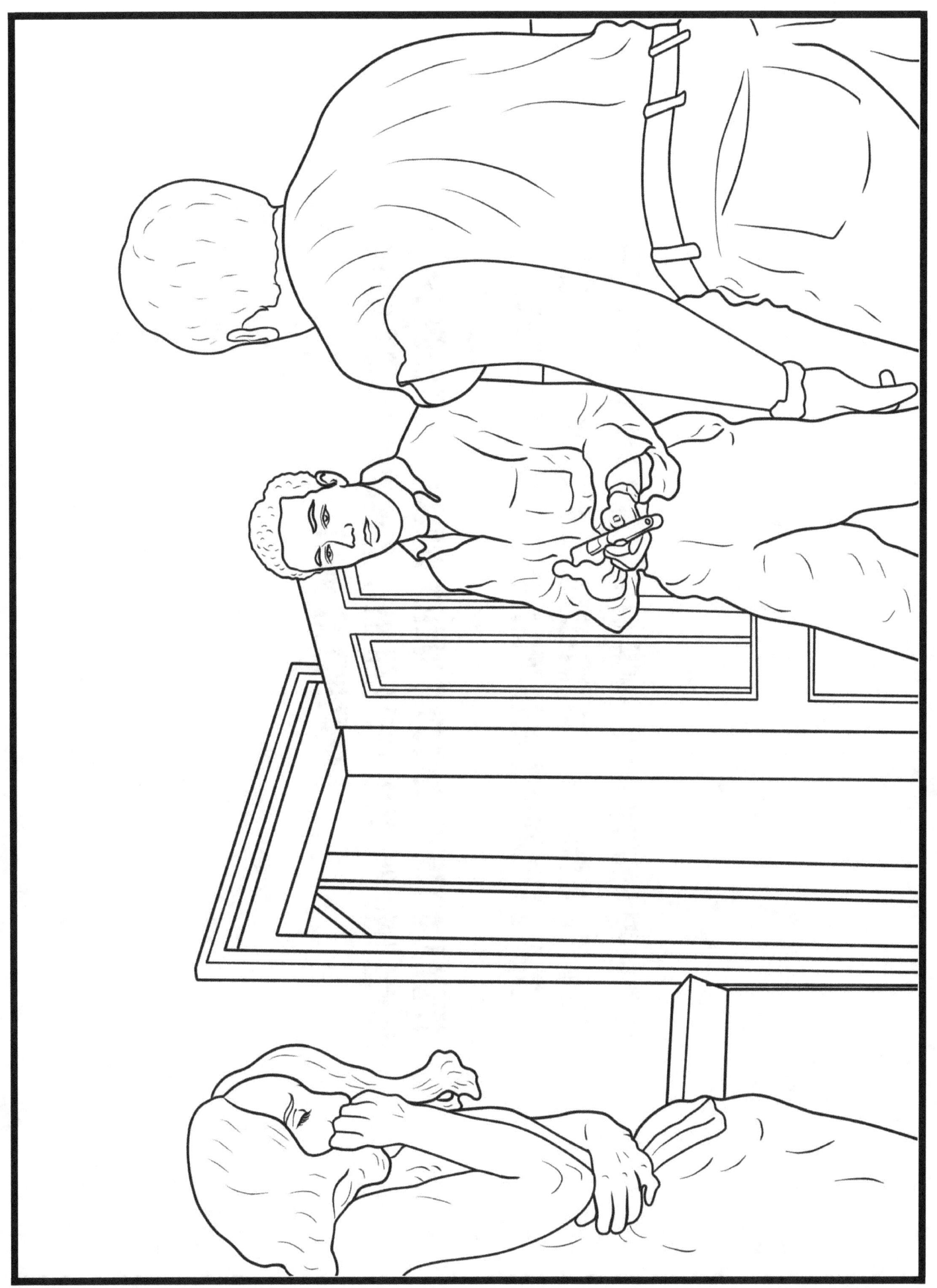

ALL 3 MEN ARGUED WITH EACH OTHER, AND MR. COOPER, THE ONE WITH A MACHETE, WANTED TO GO BACK IN THE CELLAR WHILE EVERYONE ELSE WANTED TO STAY UPSTAIRS.

THEY CONTINUED ARGUING WHILE WALKING THROUGH THE HOUSE, AND AS THEY WALKED BY A WINDOW SOME GHOULS GRABBED AT BEN!

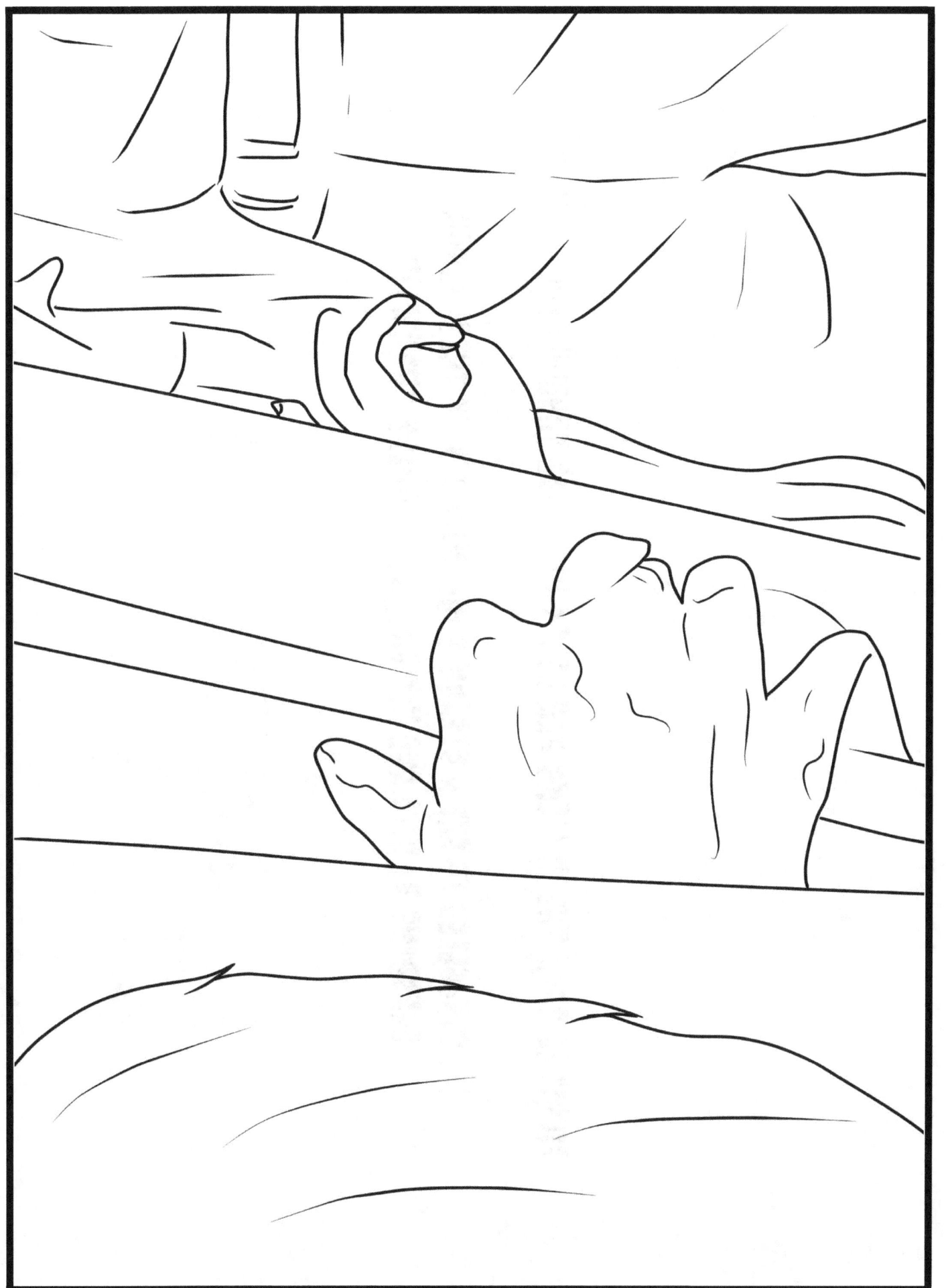

FIGHTING BACK THE ATTACKS BEN STUCK HIS RIFLE THROUGH THE OPENING

HE STRUGGLED TO GET A STEADY SHOT WITH ALL OF THESE HANDS GRABBING AT HIM AND HIS GUN, BUT FINALLY "BANG!!!"

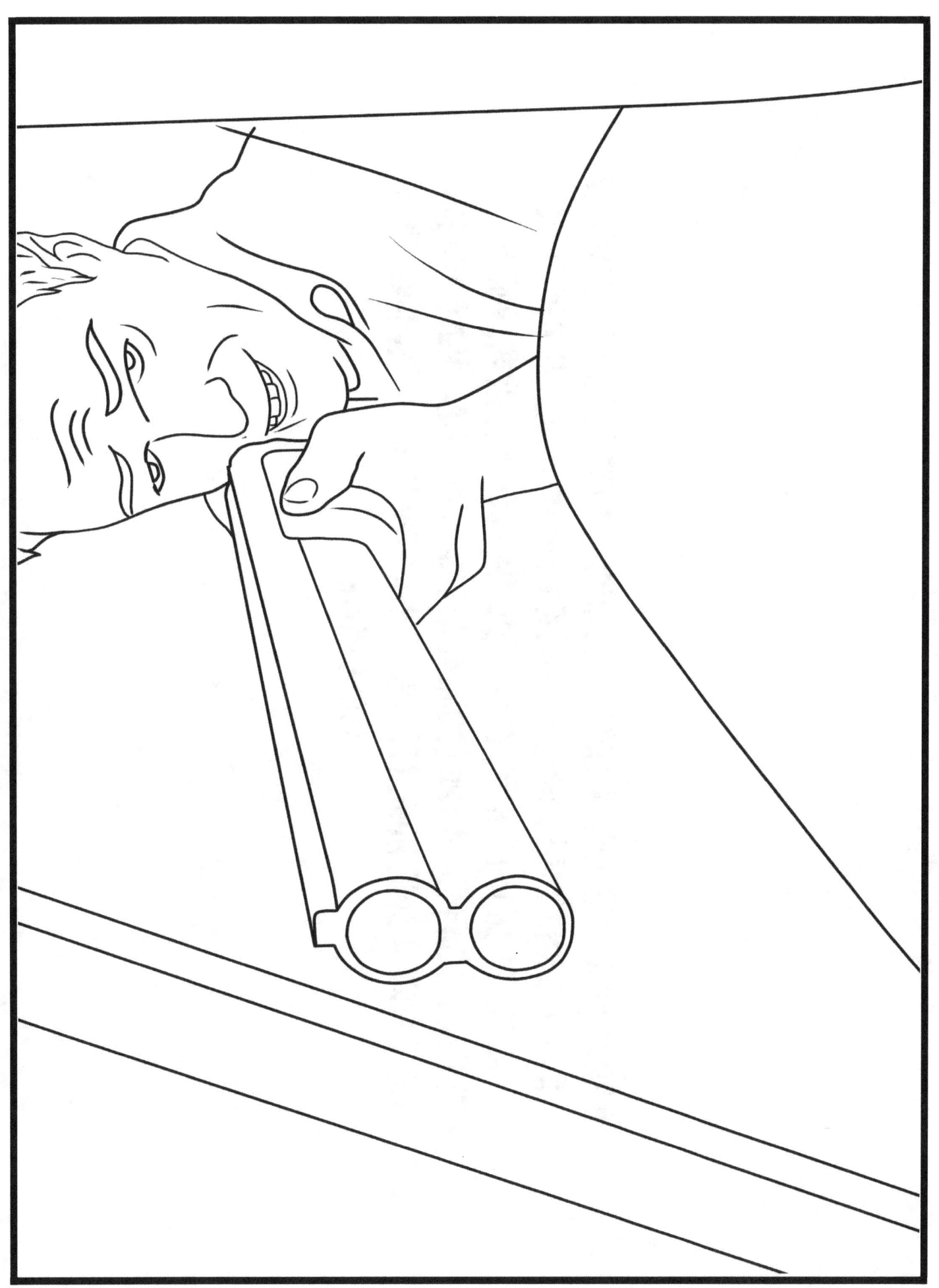

A SHOT WENT THROUGH A GHOUL, BUT DIDN'T STOP HIM! HE STUMBLED A LITTLE AND THEN LUMBERED BACK TO ATTACK AGAIN! BEN TOOK ANOTHER SHOT AT HIM, THIS TIME THROUGH THE HEAD, AND HE FINALLY DROPPED TO THE GROUND! ALL OF THOSE GUN SHOTS THOUGH WERE LIKE A BULL HORN LETTING OTHER GHOULS KNOW WHERE THEY WERE HIDING

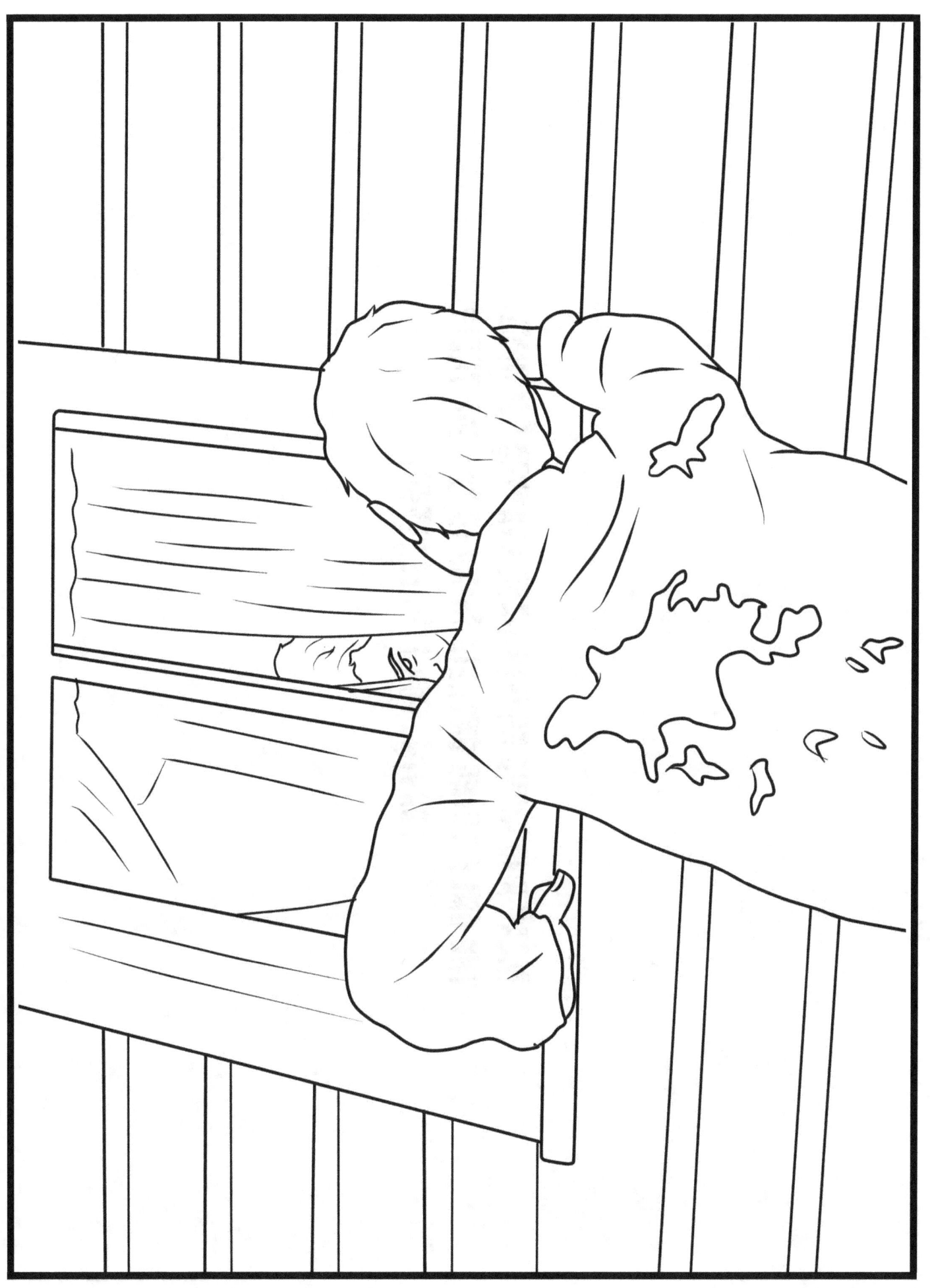

MORE AND MORE GHOULS HAVE STARTED COMING!
THE ONLY THING ON THEIR MIND IS TO FEED THEIR
CRAVING FOR LIVING FLESH!

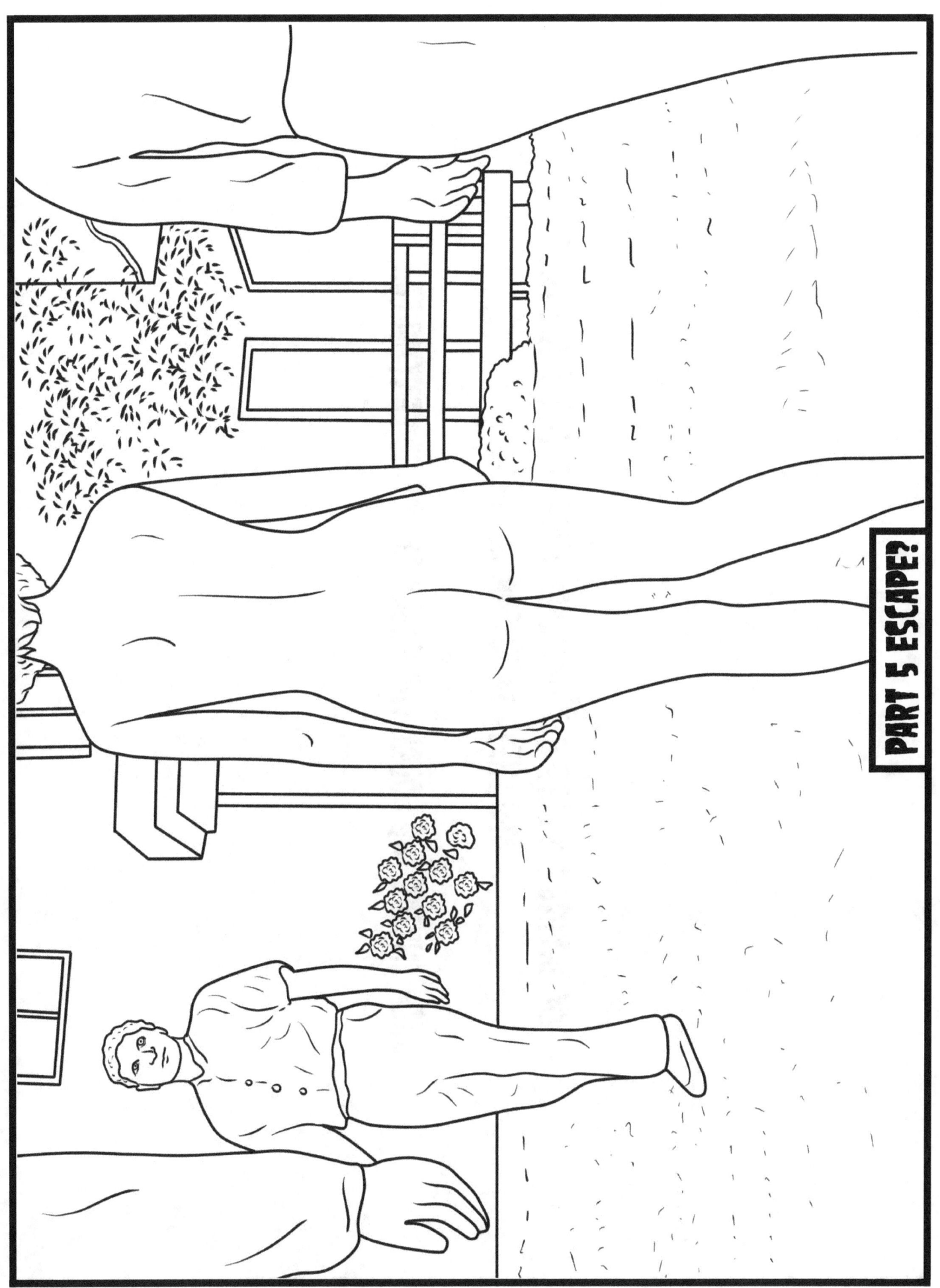

PART 5 ESCAPE?

EVEN EATING INSECTS OFF OF TREES JUST TO TRY AND STAVE
OFF THEIR INHUMAN HUNGER!

BACK INSIDE THE HOUSE THE ARGUMENTS HAD CONTINUED.....

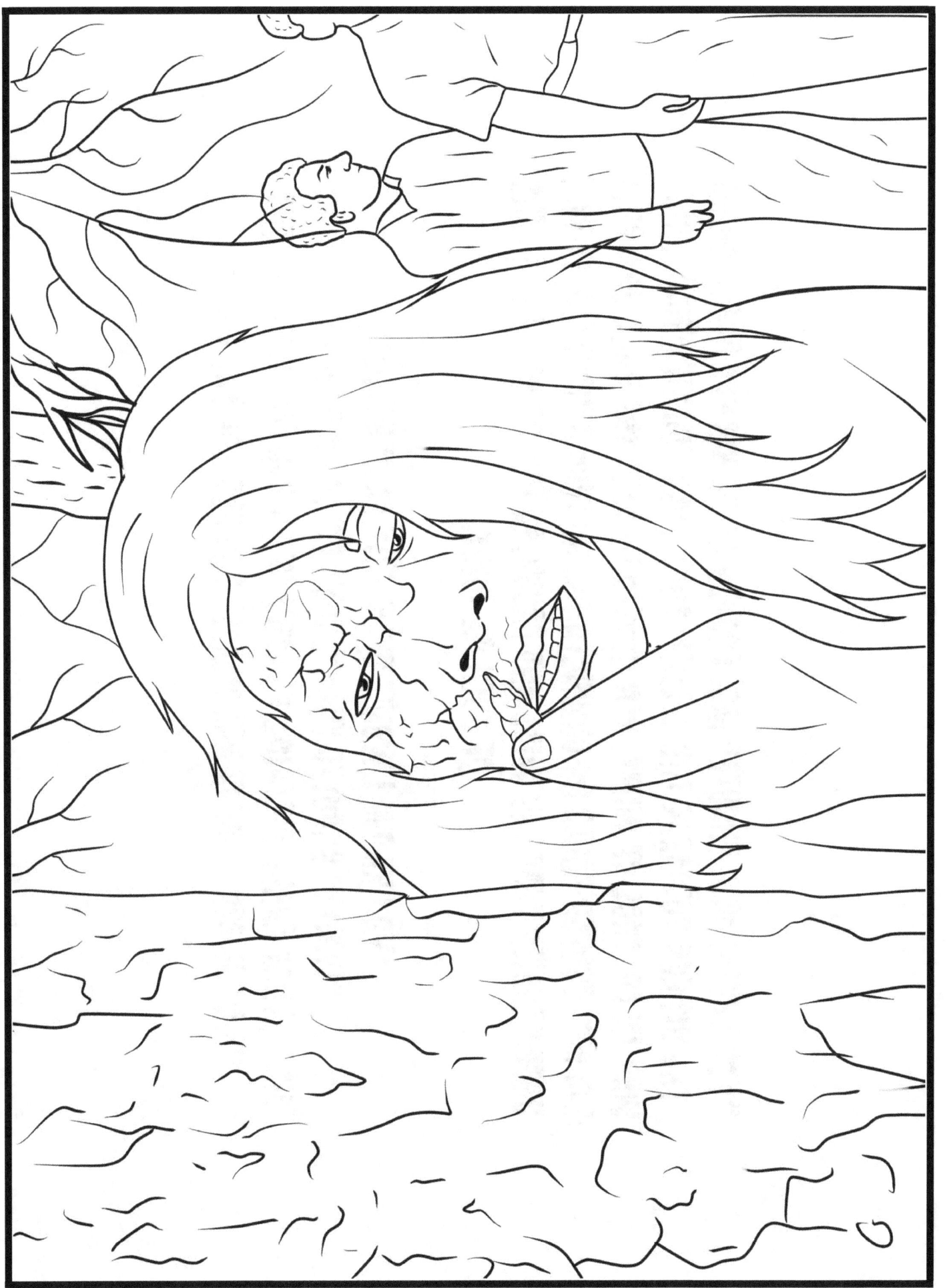

"YOU BASTARDS!" SHOUTED MR. COOPER AS HE BACKED AWAY FROM THE OTHERS TOWARDS THE CELLAR. THEY JUST FOUGHT ABOUT WHO WAS IN CONTROL OF WHAT. BEN STATED HE WAS THE BOSS UPSTAIRS AND MR. COOPER COULD BE DOWNSTAIRS. HE WAS STUPID AND IT WAS UNFORTUNATE THAT HIS WIFE AND DAUGHTER HAD TO BE IN THE CARE OF SUCH AN IDIOT.

"YOU KNOW I WON'T OPEN THIS DOOR AGAIN!"

"WAIT!" SHOUTED TOM "JUDY! COME UP HONEY!"

JUDY, THEN CAME UPSTAIRS TO STAY WITH HER HUSBAND AND THE REST AS MR. COOPER BARRICADED THE DOOR OF THE CELLAR.

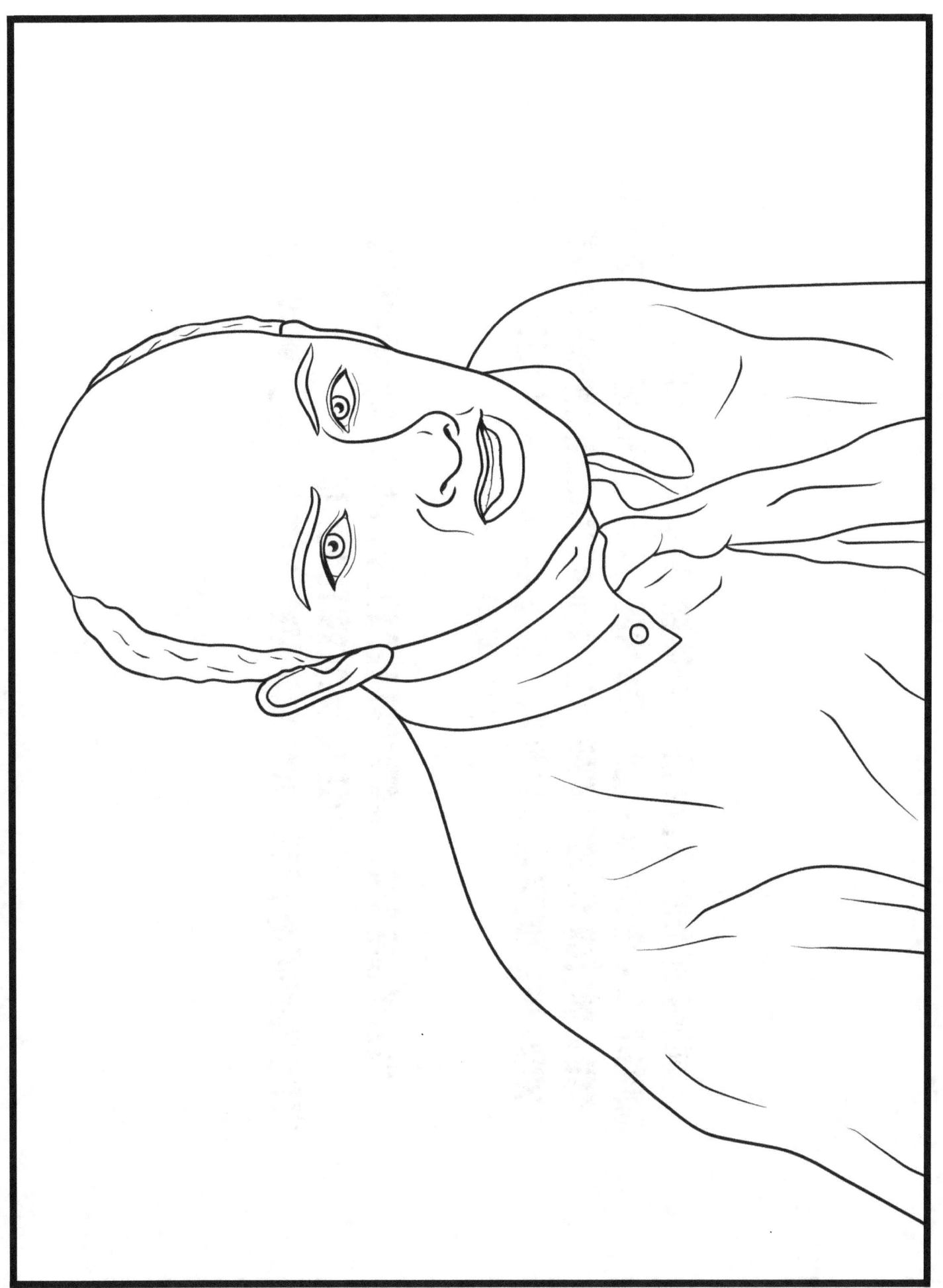

DOWN IN THE CELLAR MRS. COOPER WAS CARING FOR HER SICK DAUGHTER. SHE DOESN'T LOOK TOO WELL AT ALL. SHE REALLY NEEDS TO SEE A DOCTOR TO GET SOME HELP. AND ONCE MRS. COOPER REALIZED WHAT HER HUSBAND HAD DONE, SHE WAS NOT HAPPY WITH HIM IN THE LEAST!

"LET THEM STAY UPSTAIRS! LET THEM! TOO MANY WAYS FOR THOSE MONSTERS TO GET IN."

"IT'S IMPORTANT ISN'T IT?" SAID MRS. COOPER "TO BE RIGHT..."

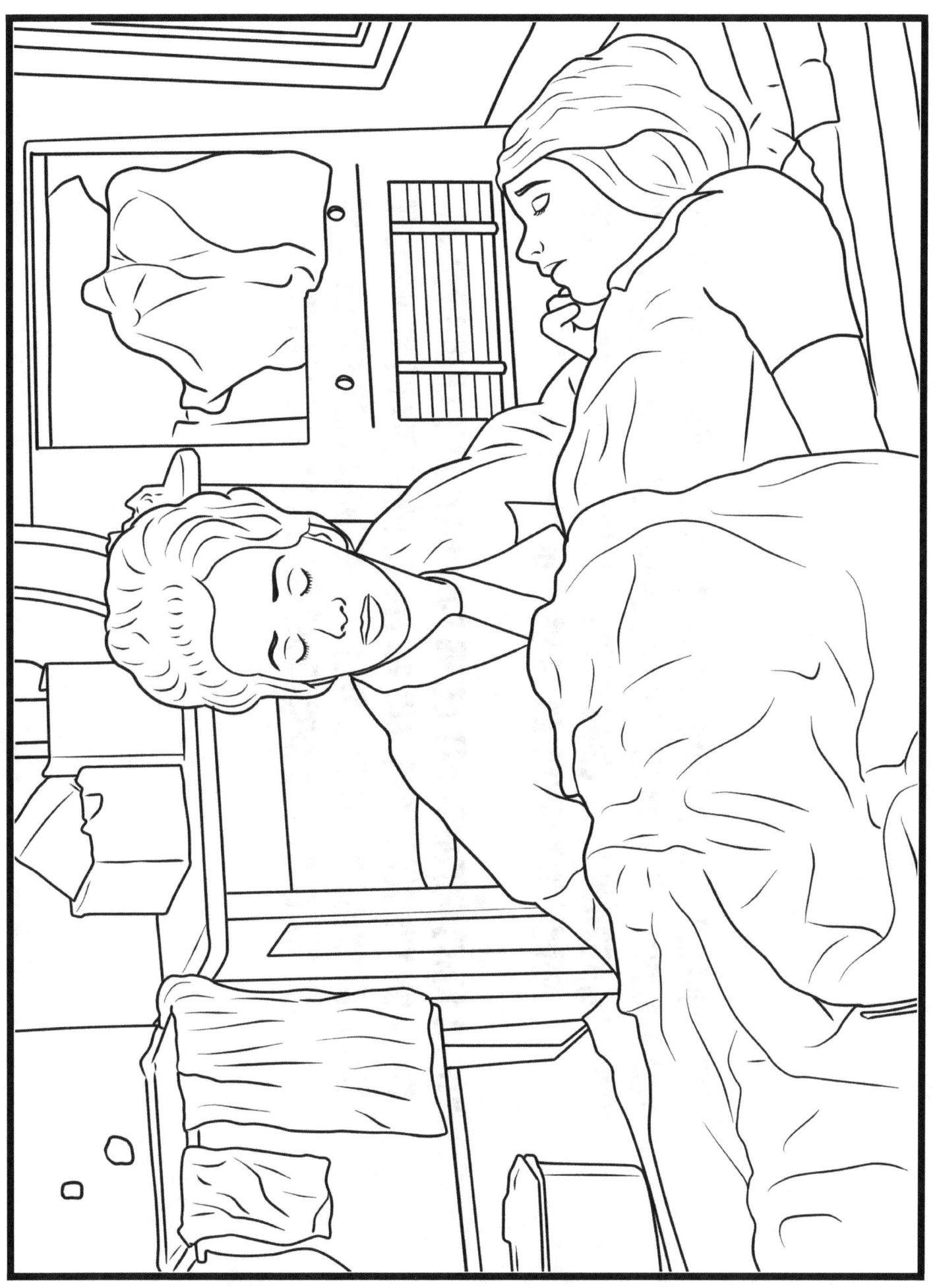

"MR COOPER," SHOUTED TOM "COME UPSTAIRS! BEN HAS SET UP THE TELEVISION!" "TOM, IF JUDY COULD COME DOWNSTAIRS AND WATCH OUR DAUGHTER WE WILL COME UP!" EVERYONE AGREED AND THE COOPERS CAME UPSTAIRS TO HEAR OF ANY NEW NEWS

"THESE MASS MURDERS ARE BEING COMMITTED BY CREATURES WHO FEAST ON THE FLESH OF THEIR VICTIMS....HARD FOR US TO BELIEVE IT'S HAPPENING BUT IT IS A FACT. IT HAS NOW BEEN ESTABLISHED THAT ALL CIVILIANS SHOULD MOVE TO A RESCUE STATION"

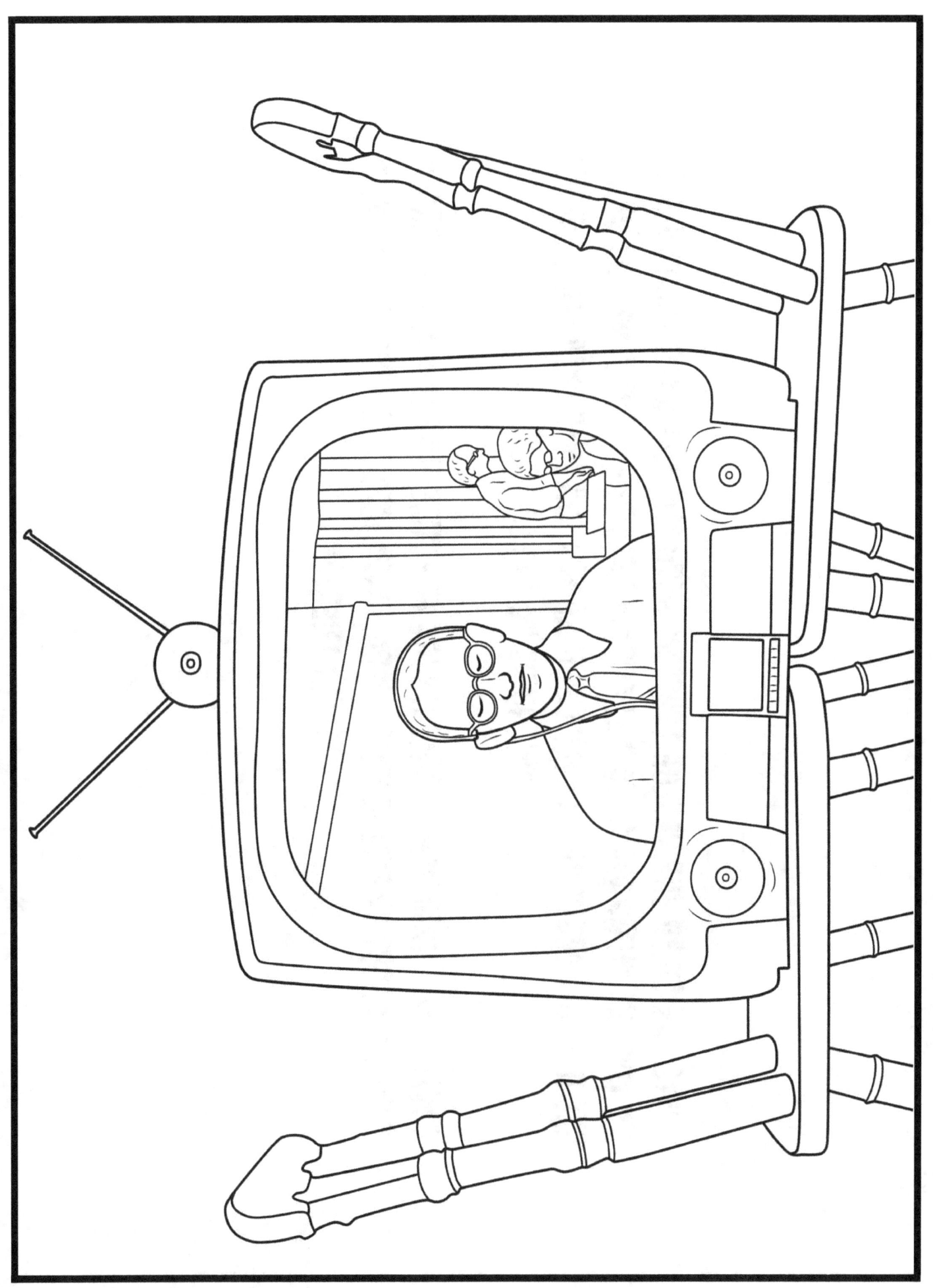

"WE CAN GO TO THE RESCUE STATION WITH THE TRUCK! IF WE CAN GET TO THE GAS PUMP WE HAVE A CHANCE!" SAID BEN "IT'S TIME FOR US TO GET OUT OF HERE!" "WE COULD GET HELP FOR KAREN!" SAID MRS. COOPER "WE HAVE TO TRY!"

"WILLARD!" SAID BEN "I SAW A SIGN FOR THAT JUST DOWN THE ROAD!" "THAT'S ABOUT 17 MILES FROM HERE" SAID TOM "WE HAVE GOT TO TRY TO GET THERE!"

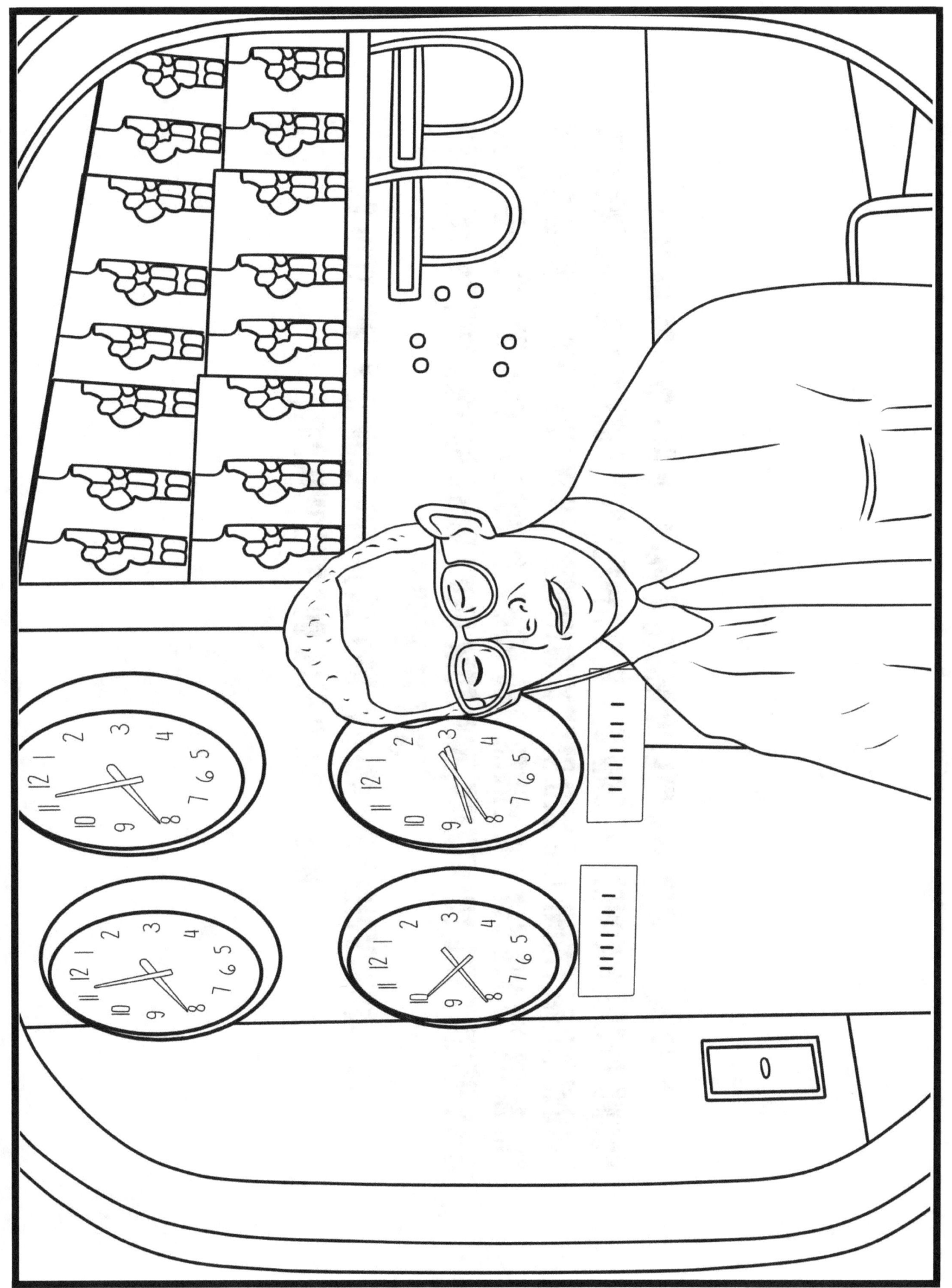

"ALRIGHT" SAID BEN "LET'S MAKE A PLAN TO GET OUT OF HERE. I FOUND SOME ALCOHOL WE CAN USE FOR MAZEL TOV COCKTAILS, AND WE CAN THROW THEM FROM THE 2ND STORY WINDOW. THAT WILL KEEP THEM AWAY FROM US AS WE GET THE TRUCK AND PUMP IT FULL OF GAS. MR COOPER YOU WILL HANDLE THE COCKTAILS, AND TOM AND I WILL HANDLE THE TRUCK. LET'S GET TO WORK"

ONCE EVERYONE WAS READY, BEN GAVE THE SIGNAL & MR. COOPER THREW COCKTAILS OUT THE WINDOW

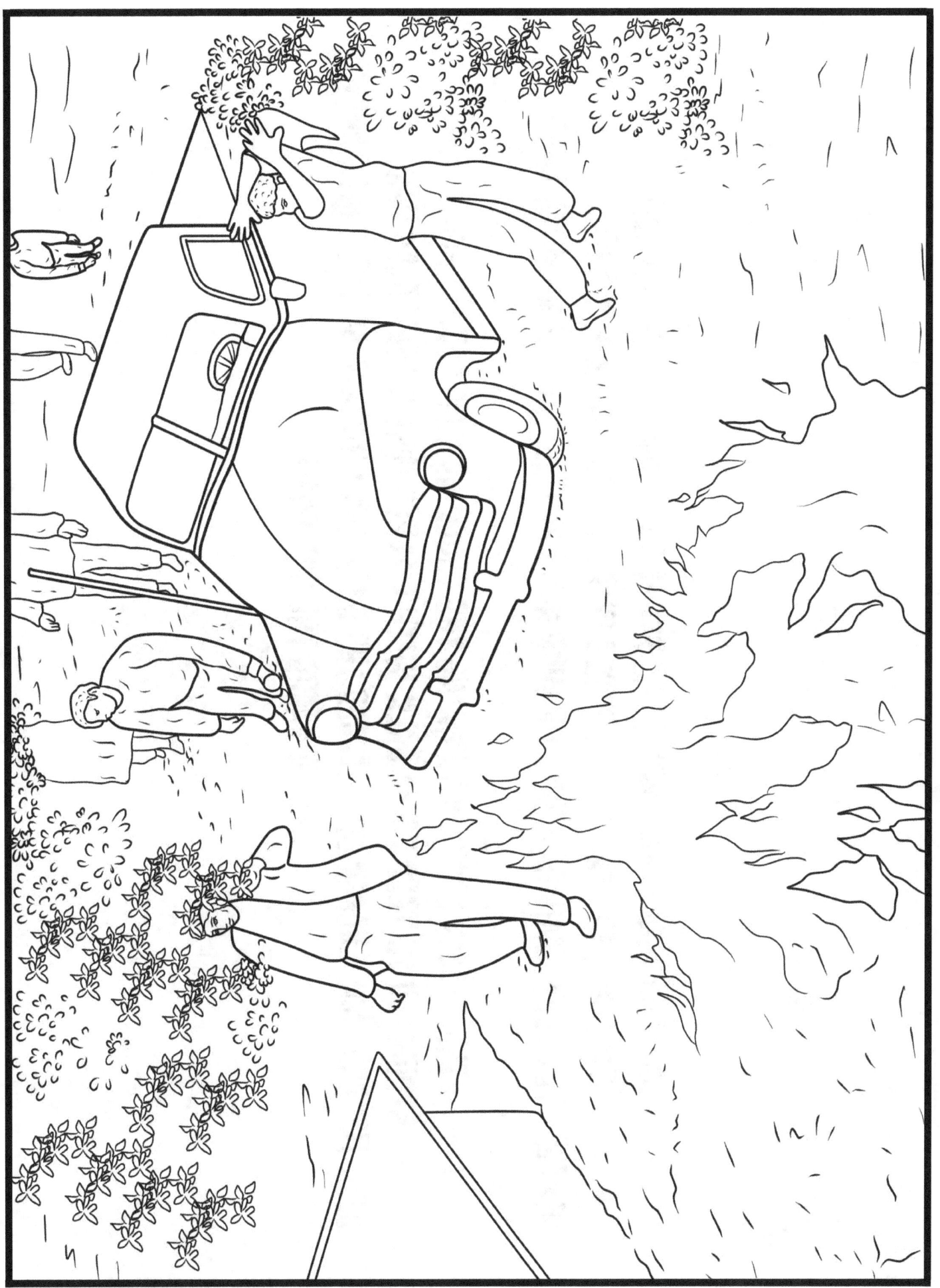

BEN AND TOM THEN OPENED THE FRONT DOOR AND STARTED TO RUN TOWARDS THE TRUCK! THE GIRLS WERE IN THE BASEMENT SAFE, EXCEPT FOR JUDY, WHO RAN OUT THE DOOR AND SHOUTED "I'M GOING WITH THEM!"

THE GHOULS BEGAN SWARMING THE TRUCK AS TOM GOT IN. BEN STRUGGLED TO KEEP THEM BACK WITH A TORCH WHILE JUDY ALSO RAN INTO THE CAB. MR. COOPER BARRICADED THE DOOR AND WATCHED AS THE TRUCK DROVE OFF TOWARDS THE GAS PUMP

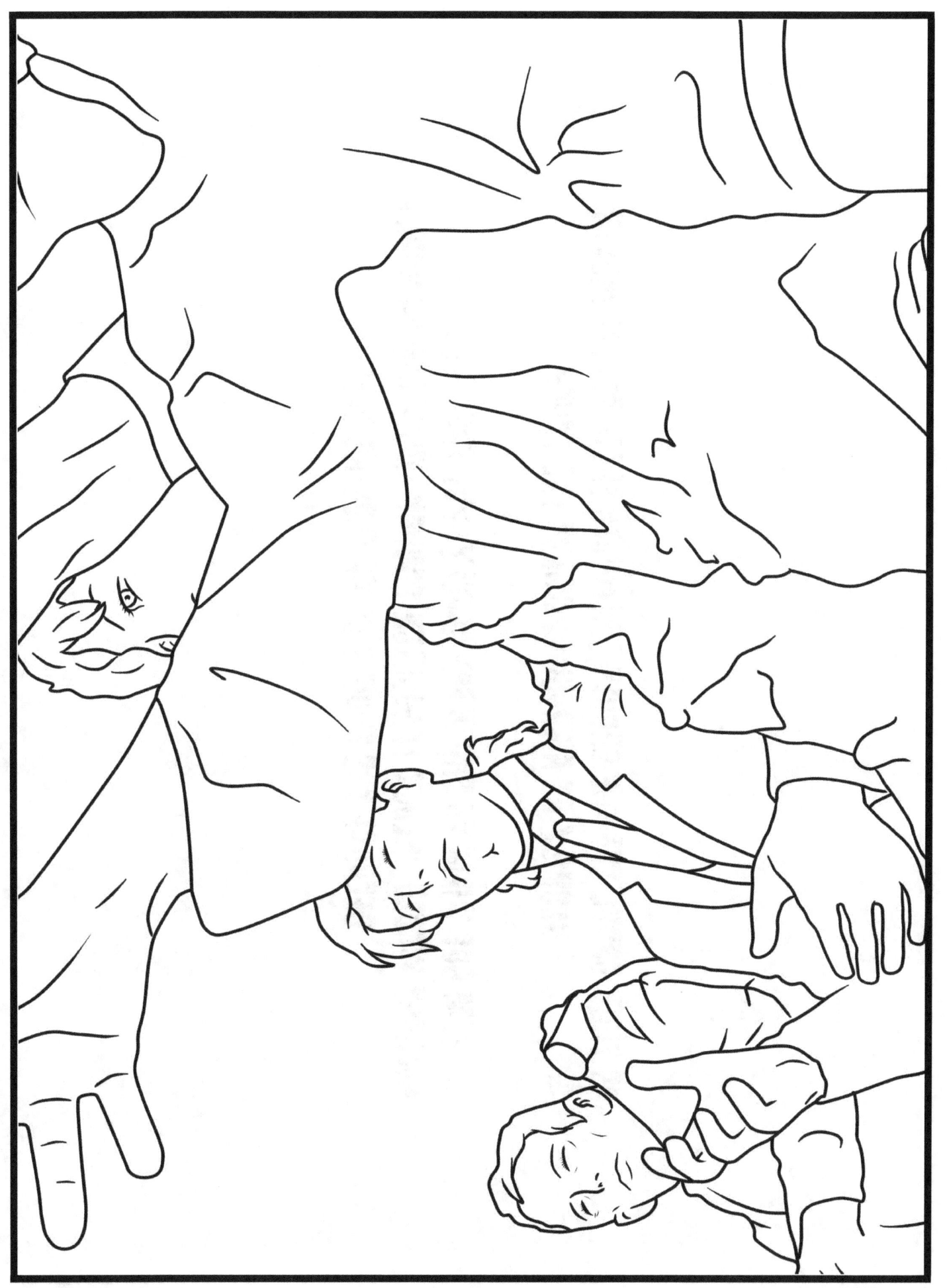

AS THEY DROVE OFF THE GHOULS CONTINUED THEIR PLIGHT MOVING SLOWLY AS A GROUP TOWARDS THE TRUCK.

TOM GOT THEM TO THE PUMP SAFELY, BUT THE KEYS THEY THOUGHT WOULD UNLOCK IT WOULDN'T WORK. THEY HAD TO HURRY BECAUSE THE GHOULS WERE CLOSING IN!!

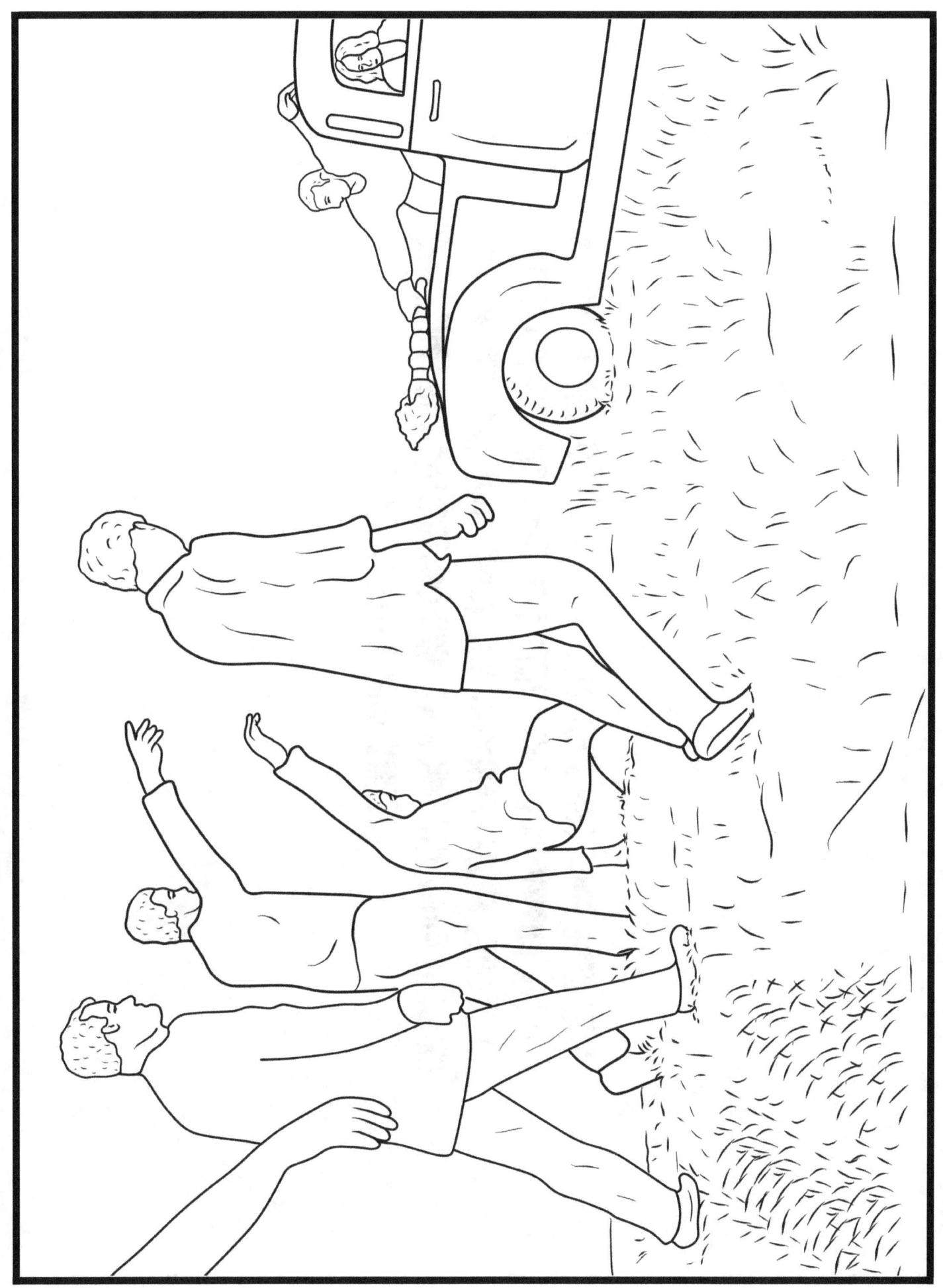

THINKING FAST BEN SHOT THE LOCK WITH HIS RIFLE. BUT IN THEIR HURRY TO GET GAS INTO THE TANK TOM DIDN'T STOP THE FUEL FROM SPRAYING THE TORCH BEN HAD SET ON THE GROUND! SOON THE GAS FIRE WAS CONSUMING THE TRUCK, AND JENNY WAS STILL INSIDE!

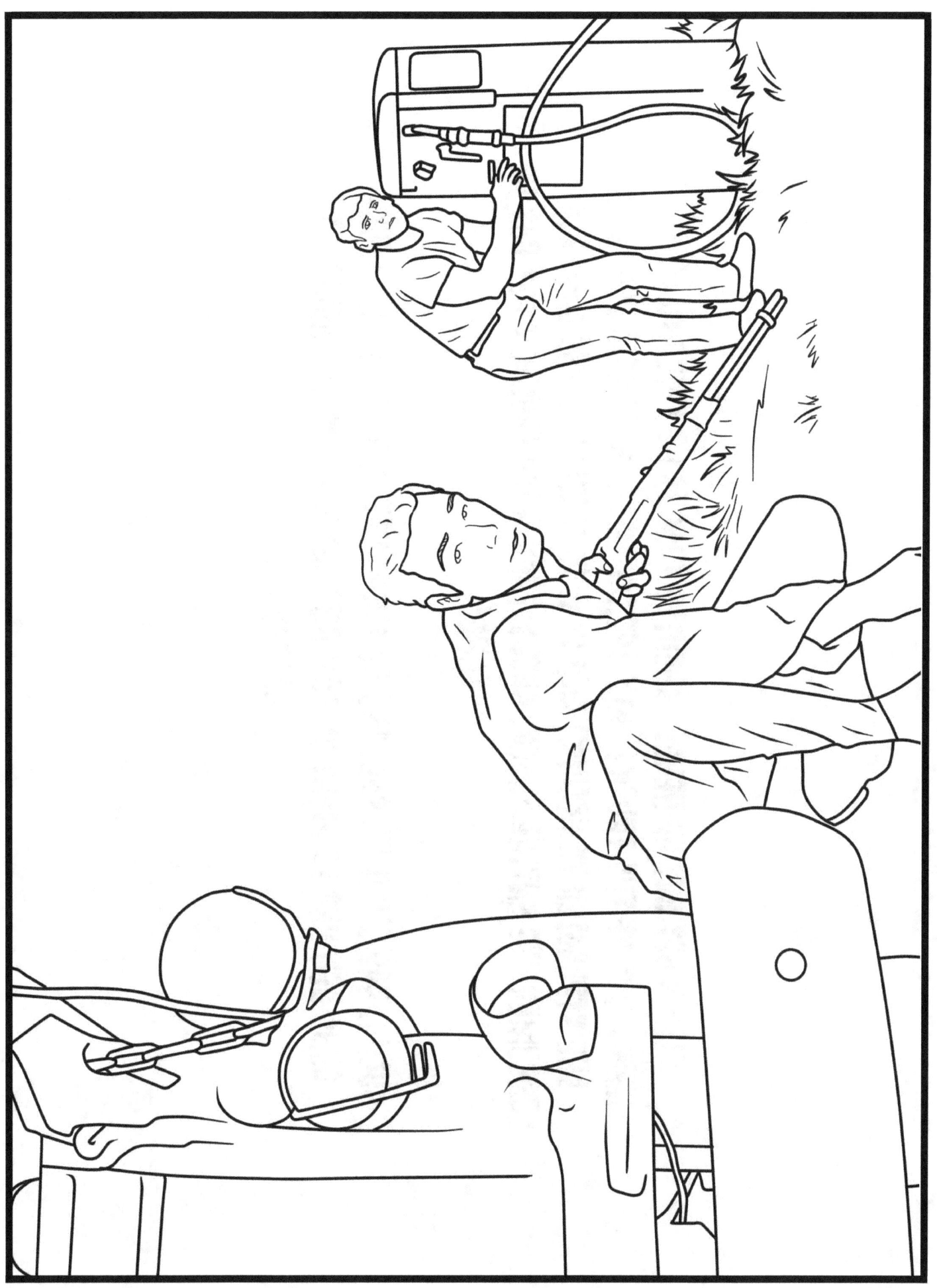

"LET'S GET OUT OF HERE!" SHOUTED TOM AS HE TRIED TO PULL JENNY OUT OF THE TRUCK! "MY JACKET IS CAUGHT" SAID JENNY AS SHE STRUGGLED TO ESCAPE! AND IT WAS THEN THAT THE GAS FIRE CONSUMED THE ENTIRE TRUCK. SADLY THEY BOTH COULDN'T GET OUT IN TIME!

SUCH A SAD SIGHT TO SEE TWO GO LIKE THAT. AND WITH THE TRUCK GONE BEN HAD TO FIGHT TO TRY AND GET BACK TO THE HOUSE TO SAFETY!

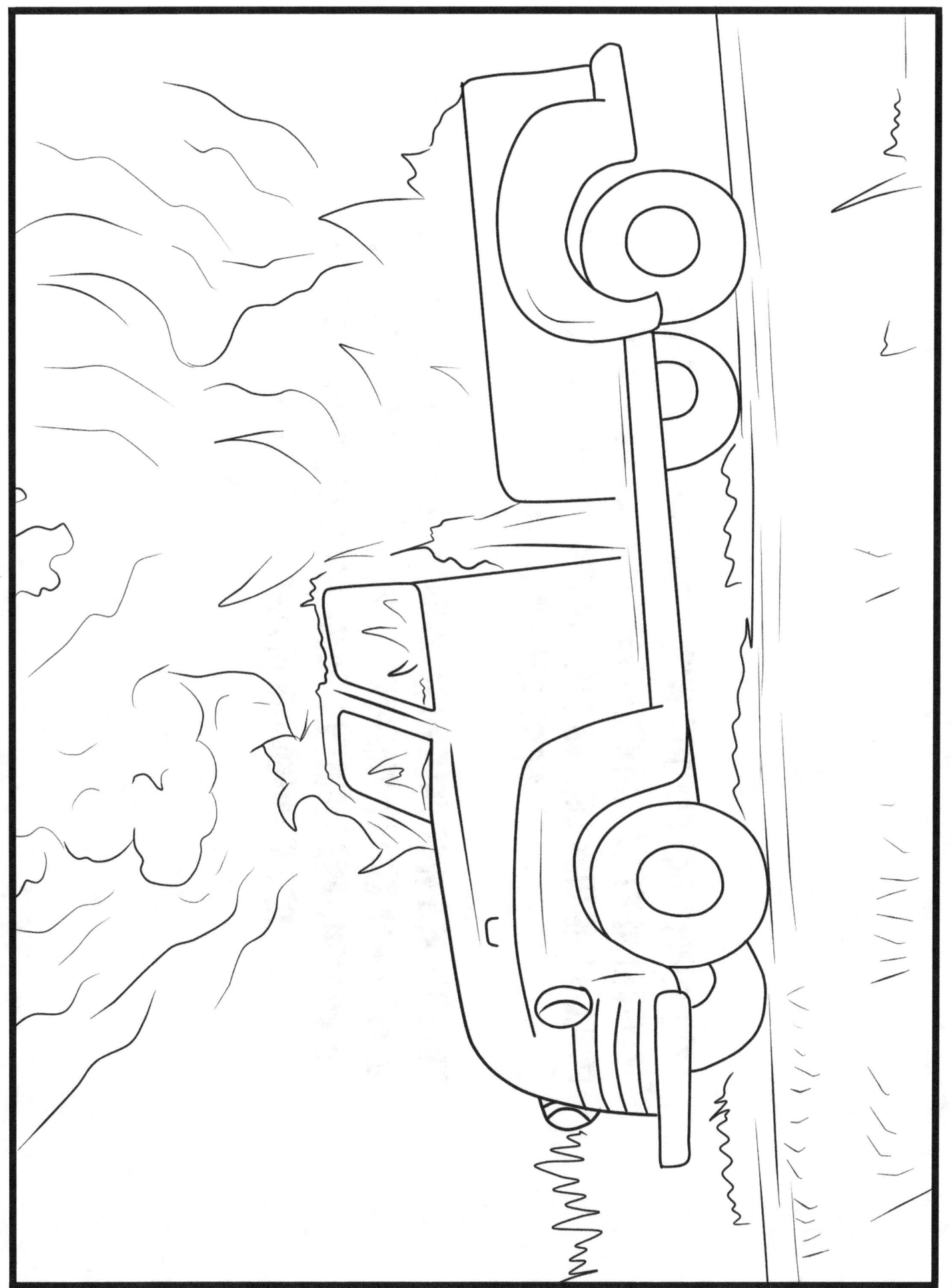

THE GHOULS HAD REACHED WHERE BEN WAS, AND STARTED TO SWARM HIM! BEN'S TORCH WAS THE ONLY REAL LINE OF DEFENSE AS HE WAS LOW ON BULLETS AND COULDN'T SHOOT ALL OF THOSE AROUND HIM!

FINALLY BEN WAS ABLE TO MANEUVER AROUND THE SWARM OF UNDEAD, AND RAN UP THE PORCH . MR. COOPER HAD LOCKED THE DOOR TIGHT AND WOULDN'T BUDGE FROM HIS HIDING SPOT AS BEN SHOUTED AND STRUGGLED TO GET IN!

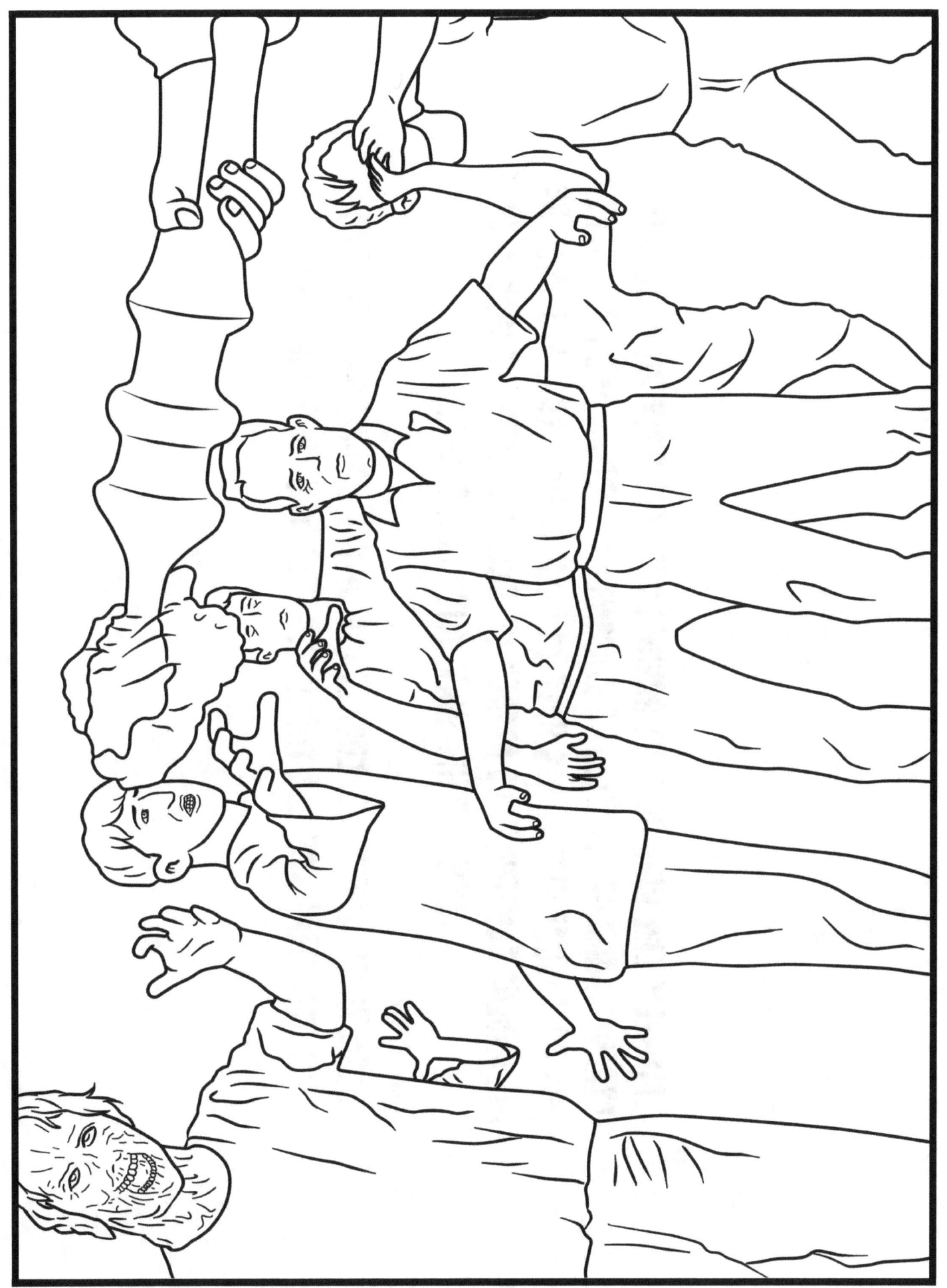

FINALLY BEN WAS ABLE TO BREAK DOWN THE DOOR WITH ALL HIS STRENGTH AND GET INSIDE. HE SLAMMED THE DOOR, AND MR. COOPER FINALLY CAME OUT OF HIS HOLE TO HELP REBARRICADE THE DOOR AS THE UNDEAD CONTINUED TO ATTACK IT. ONCE EVERYTHING WAS SECURE BEN HAD HIS WAY WITH MR. COOPER!

BEN THEN PICKED MR. COOPER OFF OF THE GROUND AND SHOUTED "I OTTA DRAG YOU OUT THERE AND FEED YOU TO THOSE THINGS!

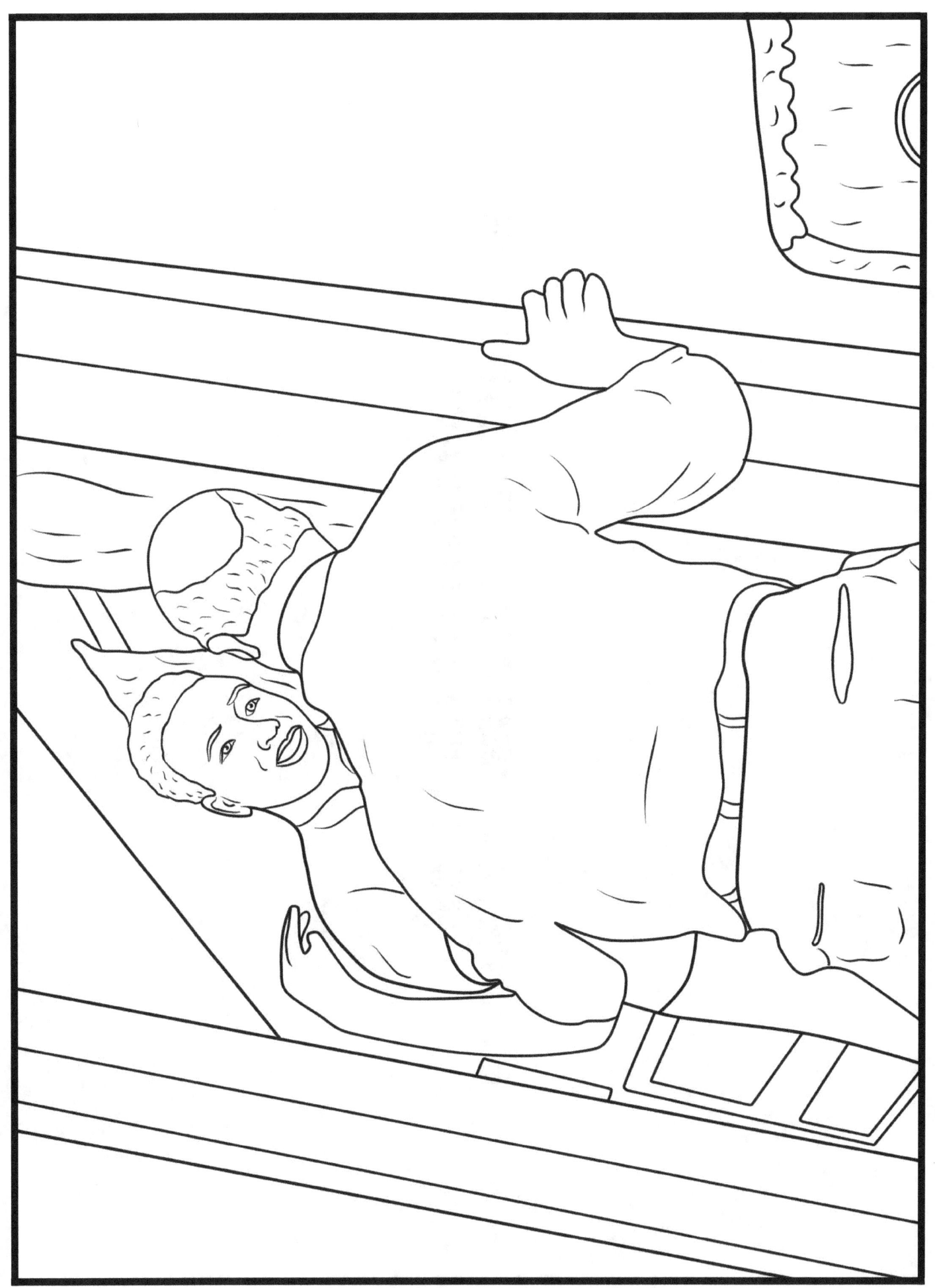

AND OUTSIDE THOSE THINGS HAD FOUND WHAT REMAINED OF TOM
AND JUDY. THEY WERE IN FOR A FEAST

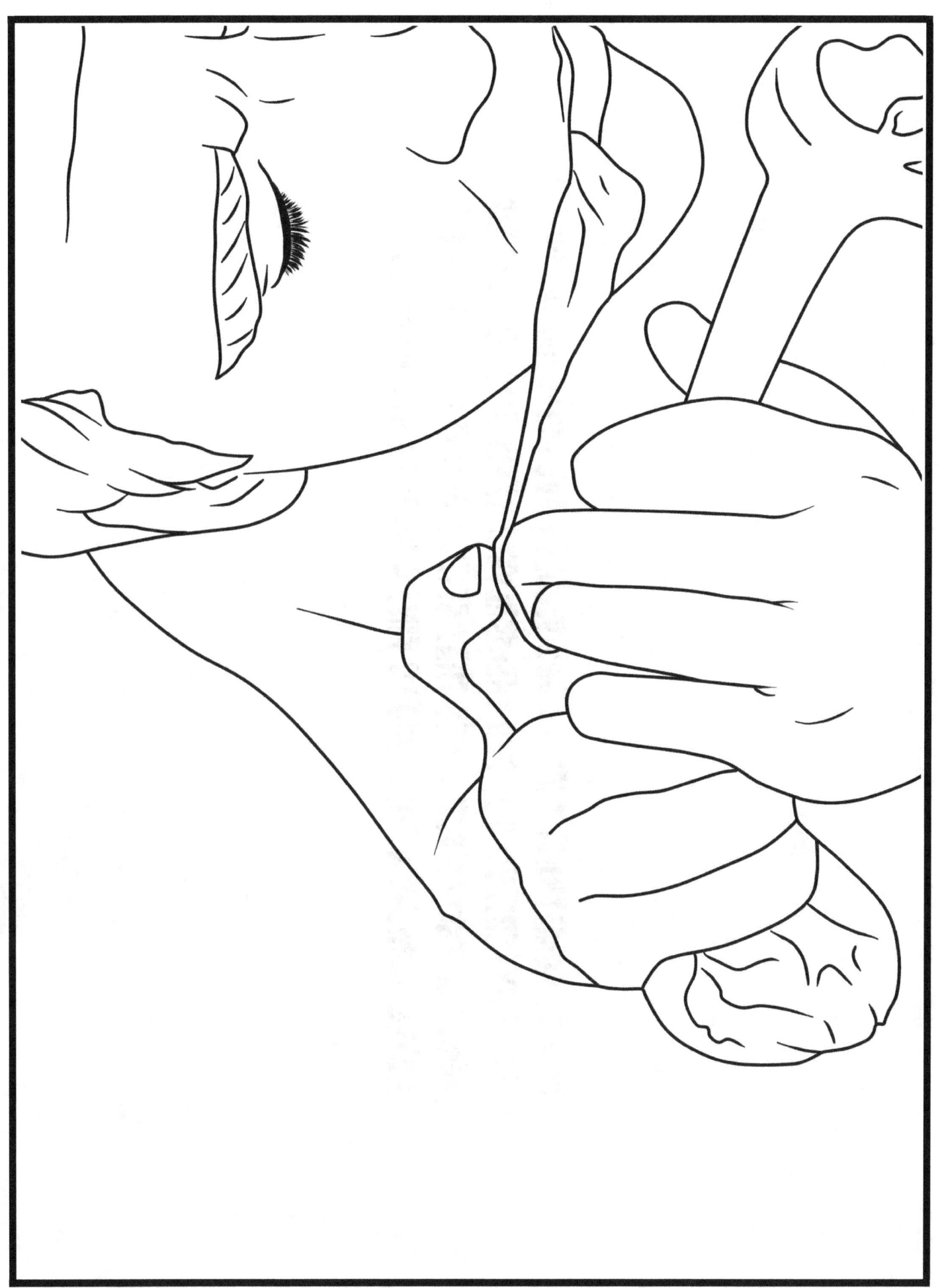

IT WAS SOMETHING THAT NO ONE WOULD HAVE BELIEVED IF THEY HADN'T EXPERIENCED IT FOR THEMSELVES! THERE HAD TO BE SOME MEANS OF ESCAPE FOR THOSE THAT STILL SURVIVED INSIDE OF THE HOUSE. SOMEHOW THEY HAD TO FIND A WAY TO GET TO SAFETY!

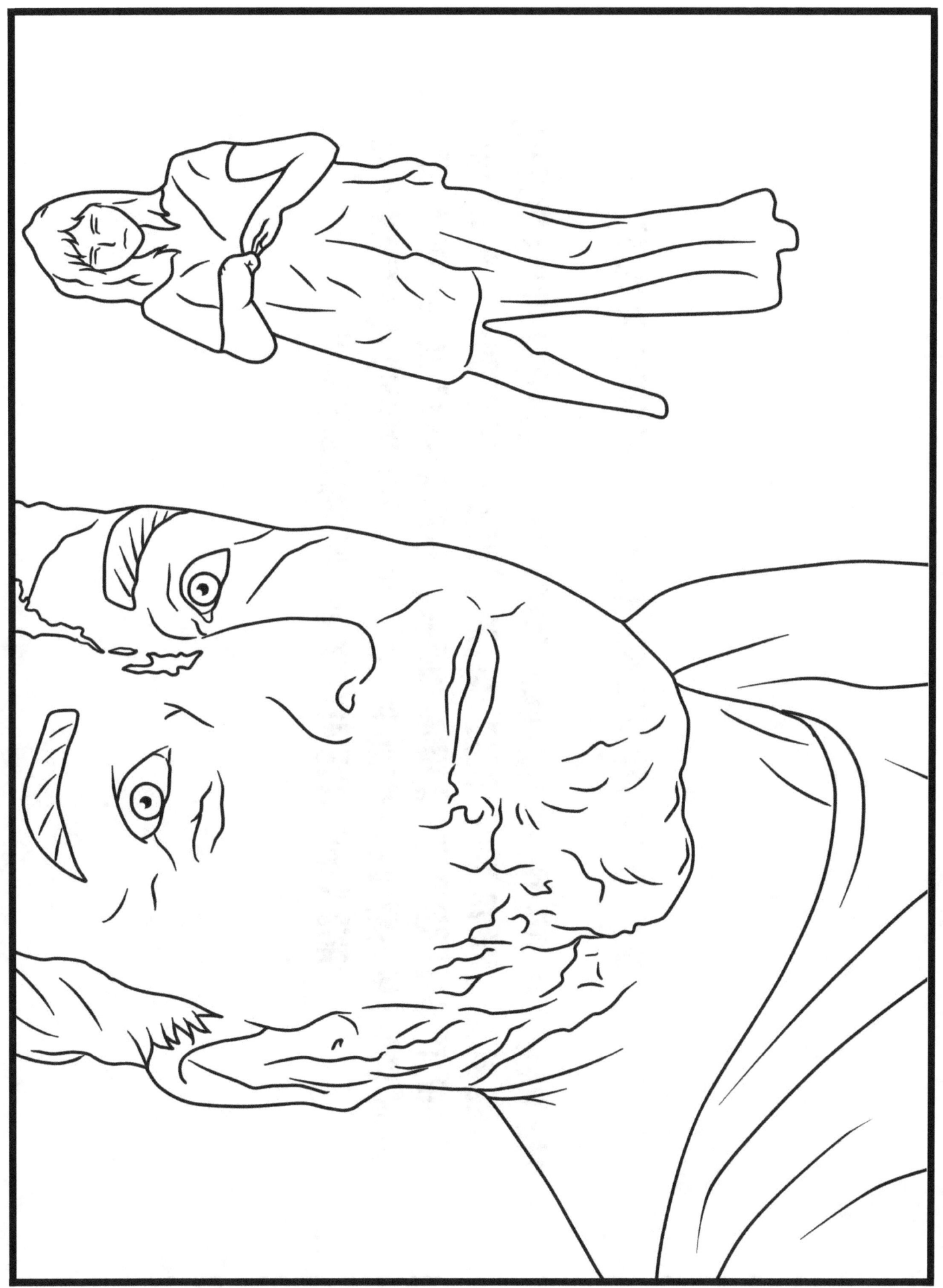

THE UNDEAD WERE GETTING MORE AND MORE RESTLESS OUTSIDE!

BEN TURNED ON THE TELEVISION AND LISTENED TO THE LATEST NEWS REPORT, "THE BEST WAY TO BEAT THESE UNDEAD GHOULS IS TO SHOOT THEM IN THE HEAD. IT WILL STOP THEM INDEFINITELY. THE CAUSE OF ALL OF THIS HAS BEEN FROM RADIATION COMING FROM SPAC..." THE POWER SUDDENLY DIED, AND A MASSIVE ATTACK ON THE HOUSE BEGAN!

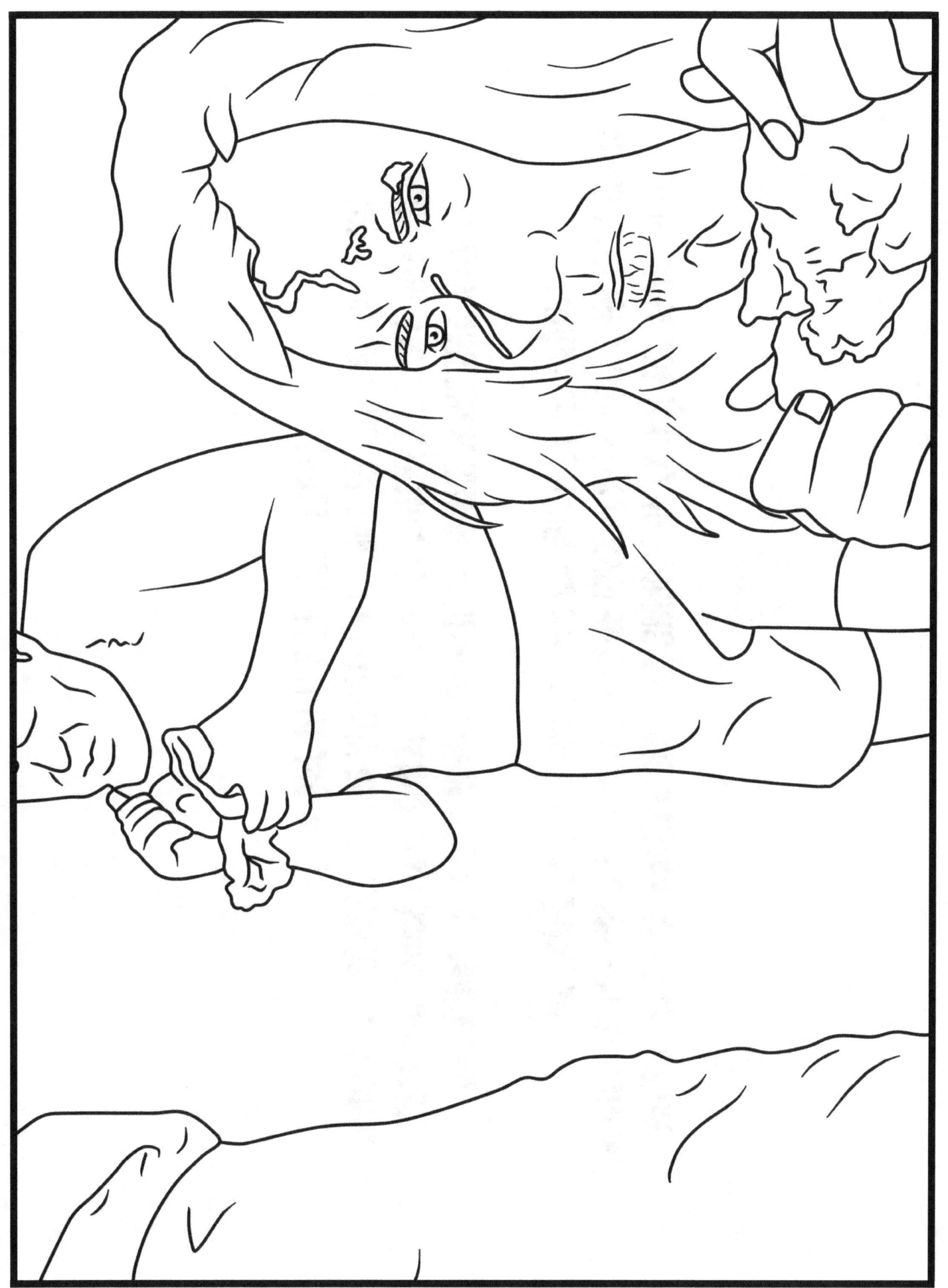

WINDOWS WERE BROKEN, AND THE SWARM OF CREATURES STOPPED AT NOTHING TO GET INSIDE! "GET OVER HERE MAN! COME ON!" SHOUTED BEN AS HE TRIED TO STOP THE GHOULS AS MUCH AS HE COULD!

HE DROPPED HIS GUN WHILE BARRICADING THE WINDOWS WHICH GAVE MR. COOPER THE CHANCE TO GRAB IT QUICKLY TO TRY AND GAIN CONTROL OF EVERYONE. "GO AHEAD! YOU WANT TO STAY UP HERE NOW?! HELEN GET IN THE CELLAR! MOVE!"

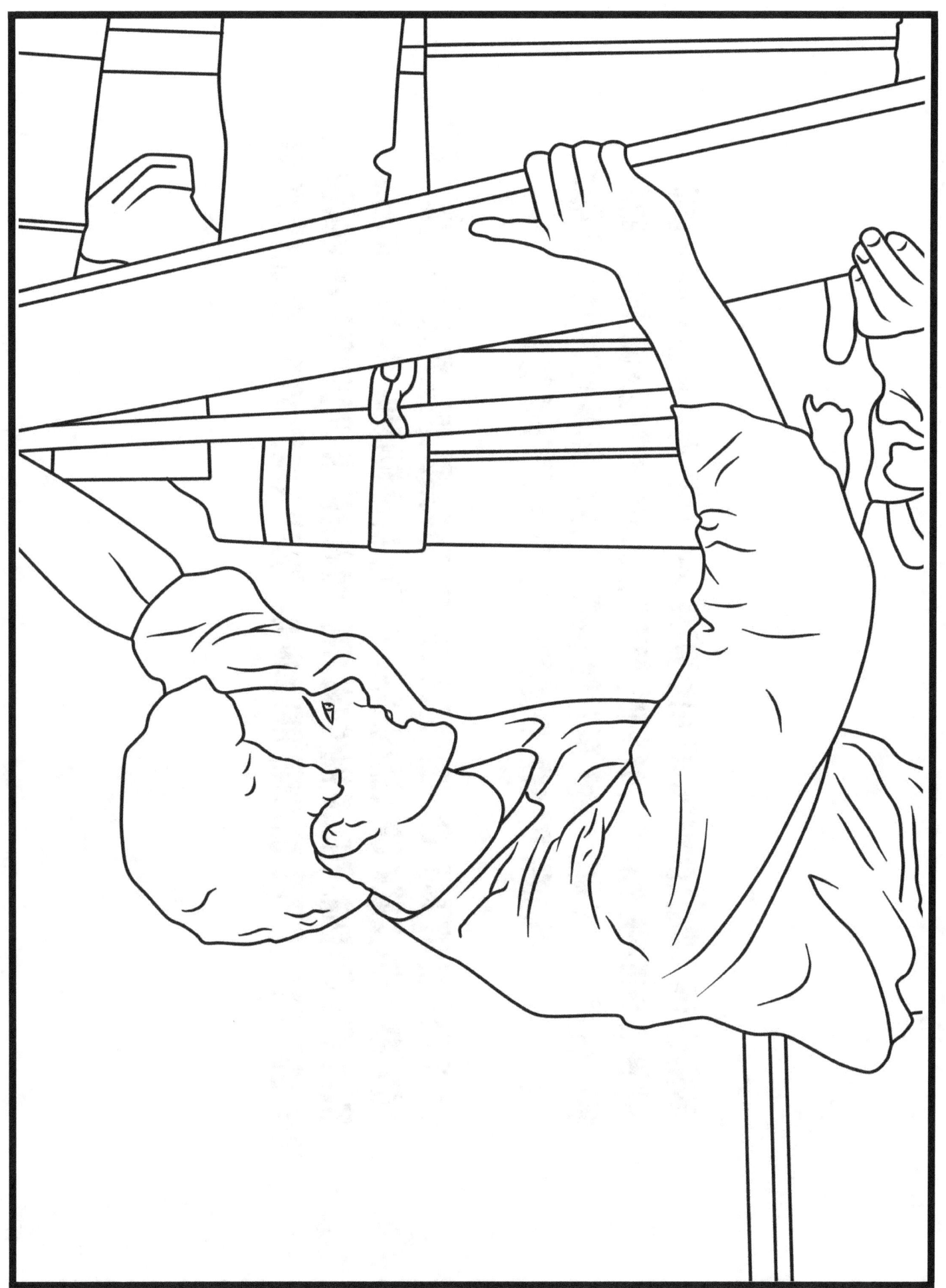

WHILE HE WAS LOOKING AT HIS WIFE BEN THREW A PIECE OF WOOD AT MR. COOPER WHICH HIT HIM AND HE DROPPED THE GUN IN A DAZE. BEN GRABBED IT AND SHOT MR. COOPER IN THE STOMACH! HE HAD HAD ENOUGH OF MR. COOPER'S IDIOTIC CHARADES!

IN ONE SHOT MR. COOPER FELL TO THE GROUND! HE STRUGGLED TO TRY AND GET BACK UP AGAIN, AND IN HIS STUMBLING, HE FELL DOWN INTO THE CELLAR. THERE HE SAW HIS DAUGHTER AND LONGED TO REACH HER, BUT FELL TO THE GROUND BEFORE HE COULD REACH HER ONE LAST TIME

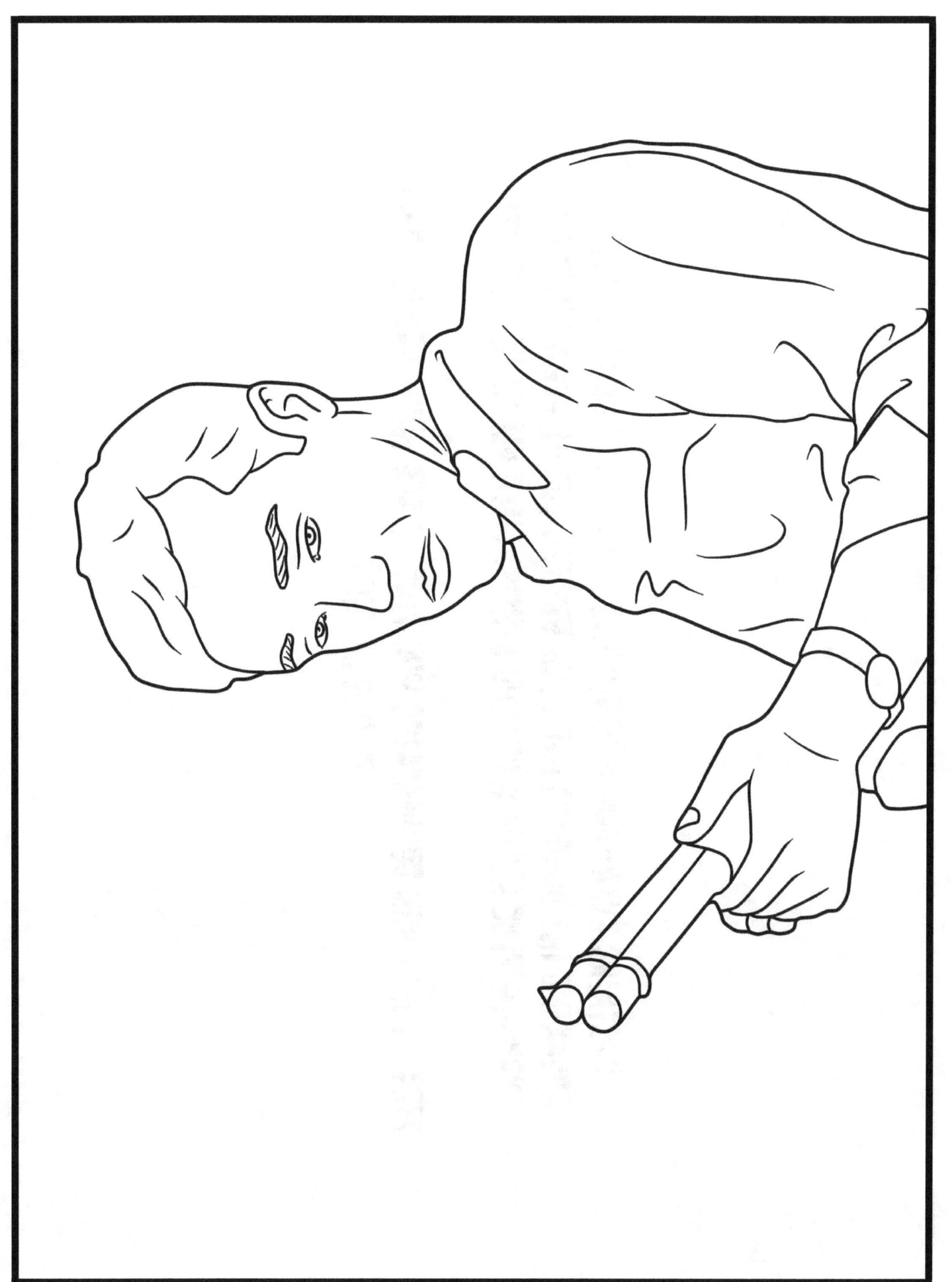

UPSTAIRS EVERYONE WAS TRYING TO KEEP THE UNDEAD FROM BREAKING IN! BARBARA HAD EVEN BROKEN OUT OF HER TRANCE AND WAS FIGHTING ALONG WITH THE OTHERS WITH ALL OF HER MIGHT!

MRS. COOPER RAN DOWNSTAIRS WANTING TO SEE WHAT HAD HAPPENED TO HER DAUGHTER.

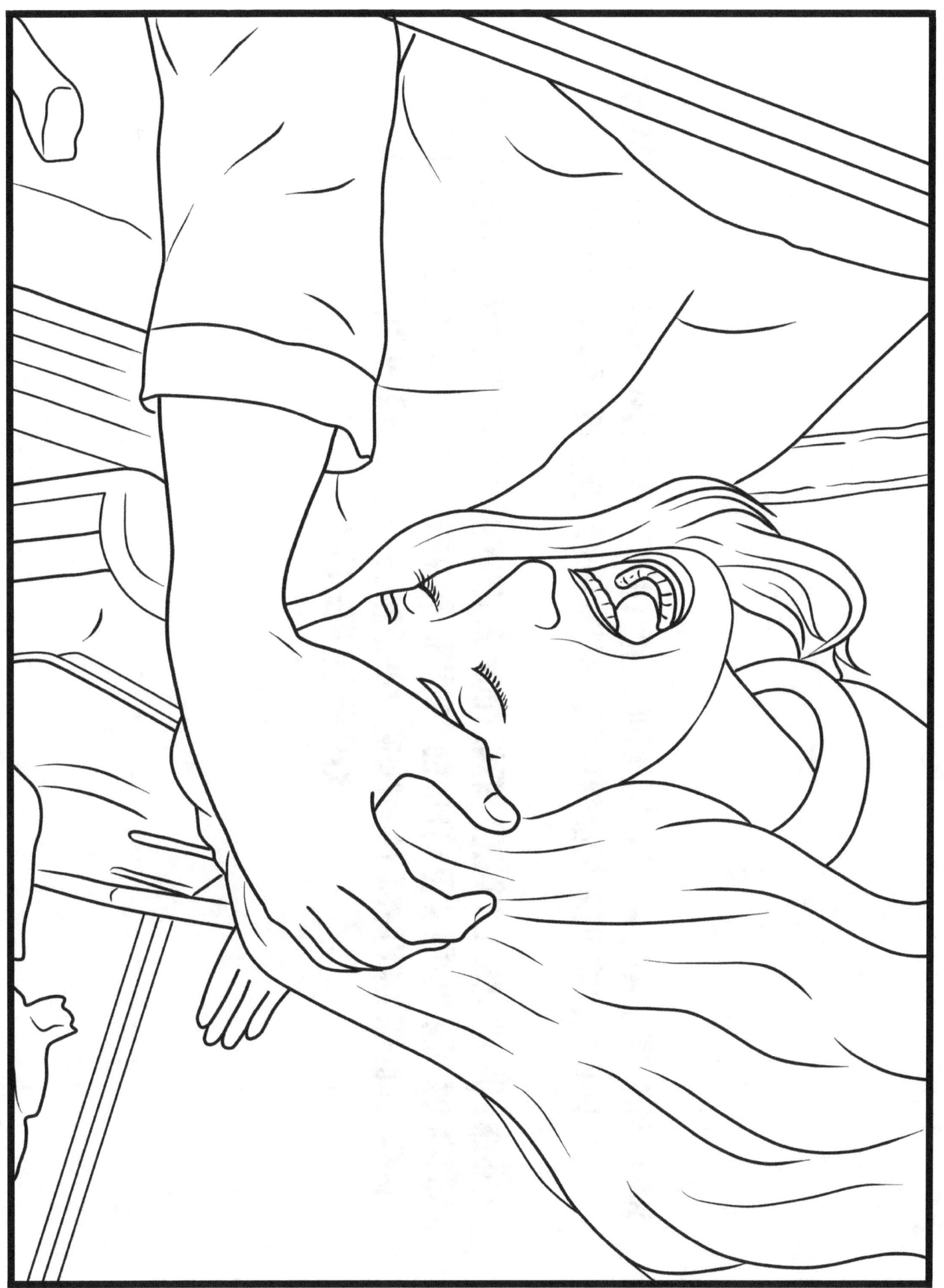

WHAT SHE SAW WAS NOT AT ALL WHAT SHE COULD HAVE EVER IMAGINED! KNEELING DOWN NEAR HER DEAD FATHER, KAREN WAS FEASTING ON HIS FLESH!

"KAREN! OH KAREN....." CRIED MRS. COOPER. KAREN TURNED TO MRS. COOPER AT THE SOUND OF HER VOICE AND STARTED COMING TOWARDS HER! "OH BABY....." SOBBED MRS. COOPER AS KAREN CONTINUED TOWARDS HER MOTHER WITH THE LOOK OF A KILLER IN HER EYES

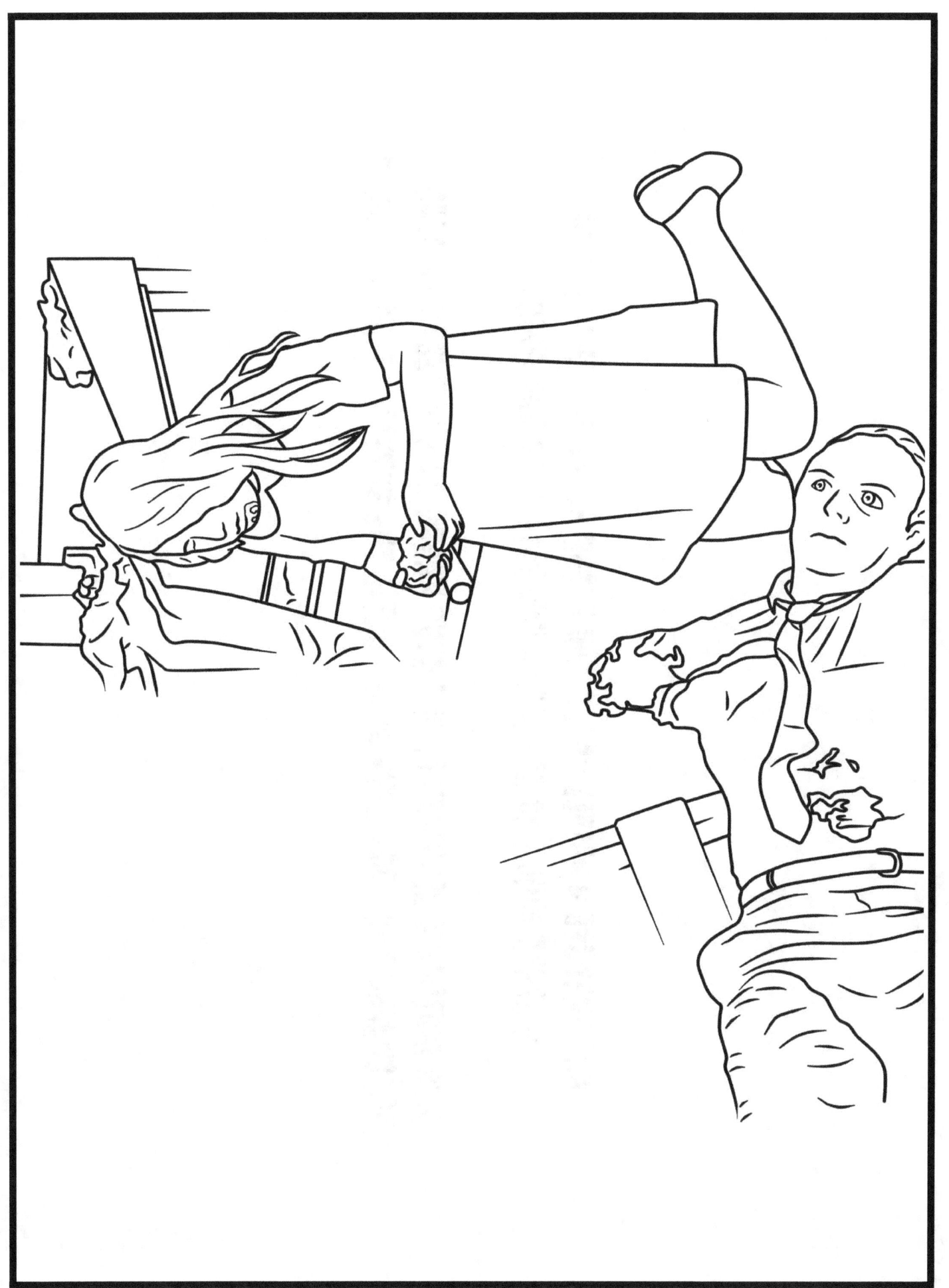

SHE GRABBED A SMALL SPADE AND BEGAN MOVING TOWARDS HER MOTHER WHO HAD STUMBLED AND FALLEN TO THE GROUND.

HER MOTHER'S SCREAMS DIDN'T STOP KAREN AS SHE BEGAN TO STAB MRS. COOPER OVER AND OVER AGAIN UNTIL THE SCREAMS FINALLY ENDED.

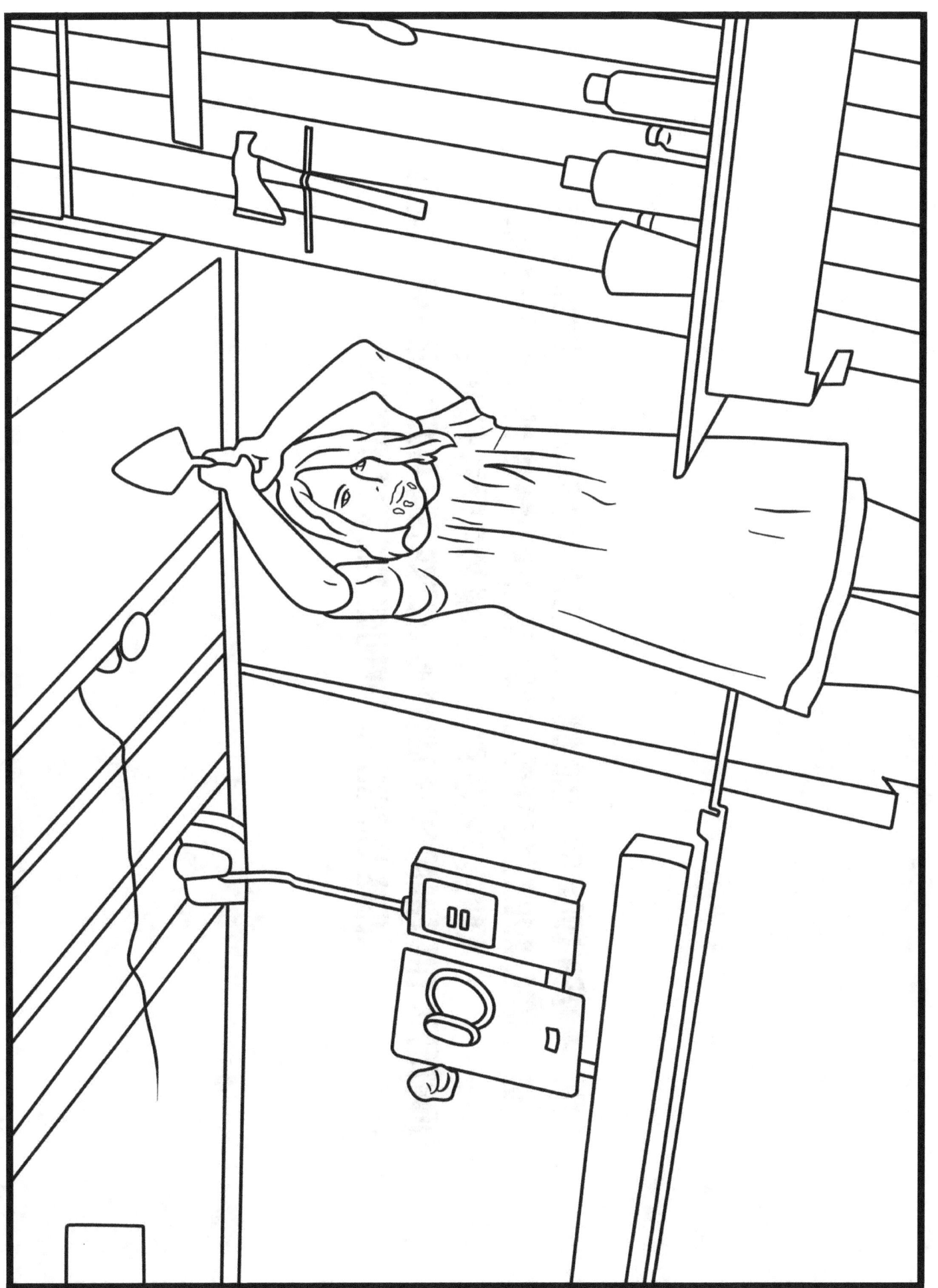

THE FROZEN LOOK OF FEAR ON HER MOTHER'S FACE, THE COMMOTION UPSTAIRS, AND THE BLOOD COVERING HER HANDS DID NOT DISSUADE KAREN FROM FEASTING ON HER FRESH KILL.

UPSTAIRS THE CHAOS WAS GETTING WORSE AND WORSE AS THE UNDEAD WERE BREAKING THROUGH THE BARRICADES!

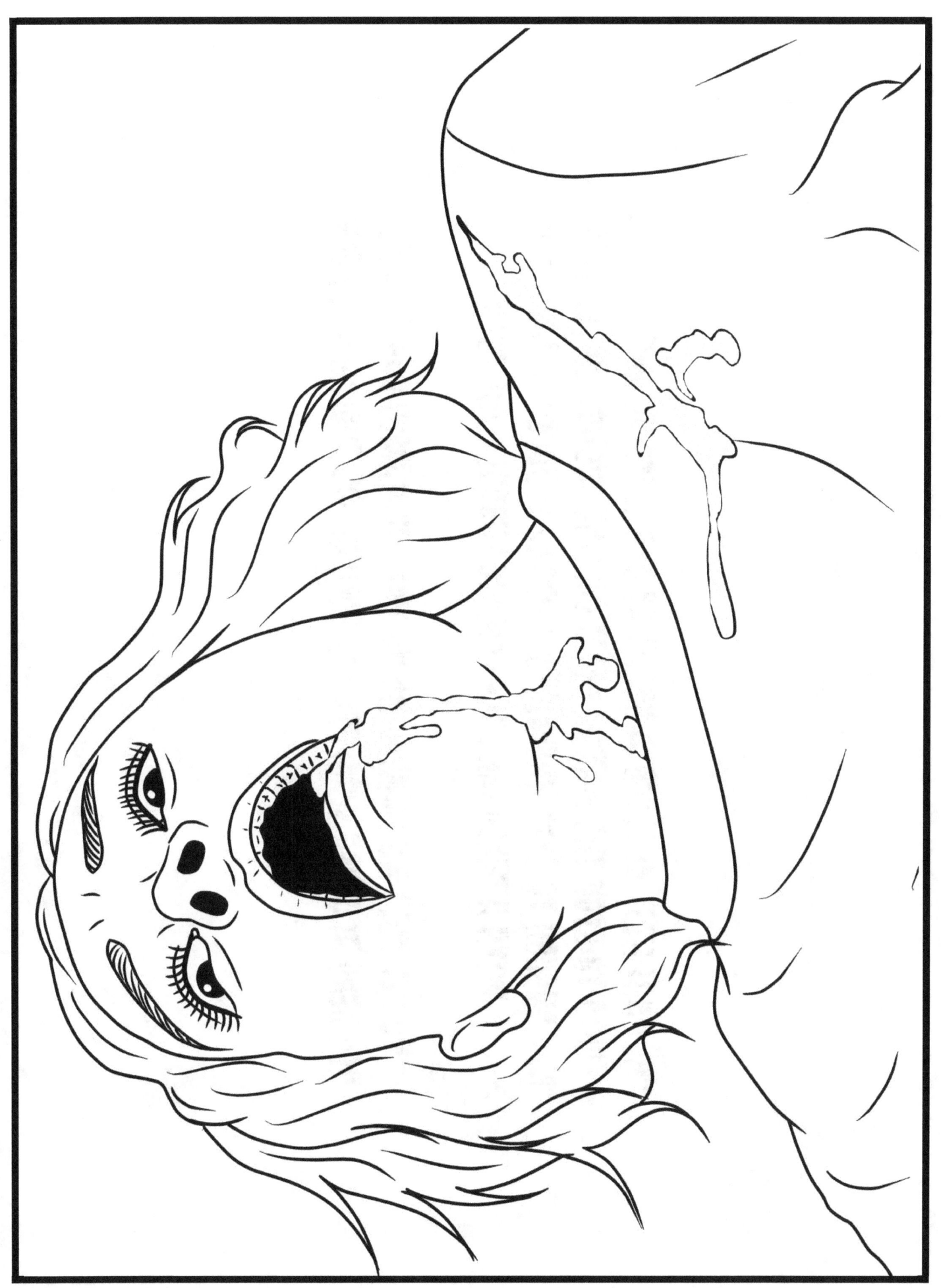

"NO! NO! NO!" SHOUTED BARBARA AS SHE TRIED AS MUCH AS SHE COULD TO STOP THE UNDEAD FROM COMING INSIDE. BUT IT WAS NOT ENOUGH TO STOP THEM. THEY BROKE THROUGH STRONGHOLD, WITH A FAMILIAR FACE COMING THROUGH THE DOOR

"NO GET OUT! NO JOHNNY NO NO NO!" SCREAMED BARABRA AS HER DEAD BROTHER WRAPPED HIS COLD HANDS AROUND HER NECK

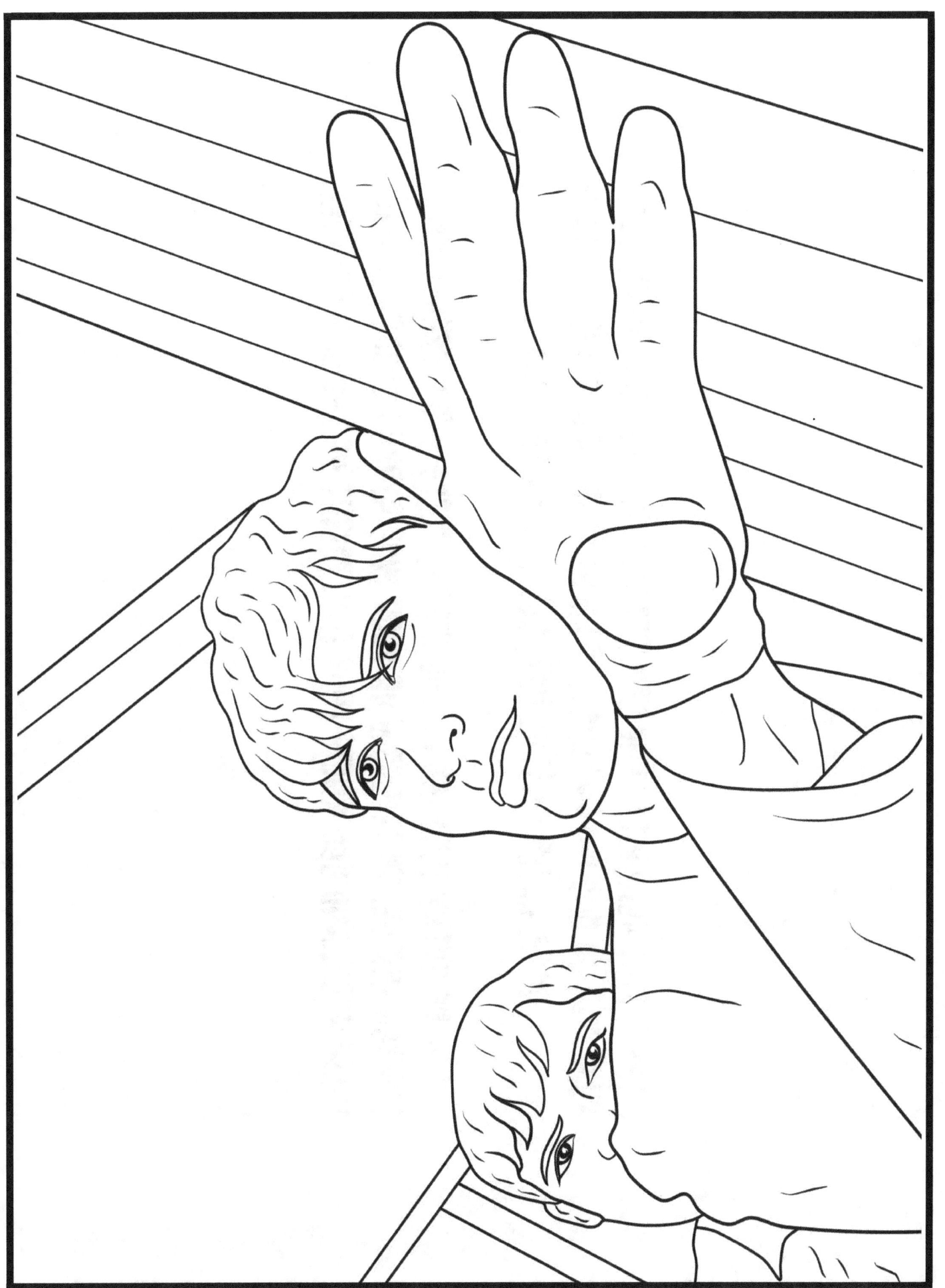

"HELP ME! HELP ME! HELP ME!" SHE SCREAMED AS THE SWARM OF GHOULS TOOK HER UP AND BEGAN FEASTING ON HER. BEN HAD TRIED AS MUCH AS HE COULD TO SAVE HER, BUT IT WAS TOO LATE....

OUT OF EVERY OPENING OF THE HOUSE, THERE WERE CREATURES COMING INSIDE. NO WINDOW OR DOOR WAS STRONG ENOUGH TO HOLD THEM BACK, AND BEN KNEW THAT THIS MIGHT BE THE END FOR HIM.

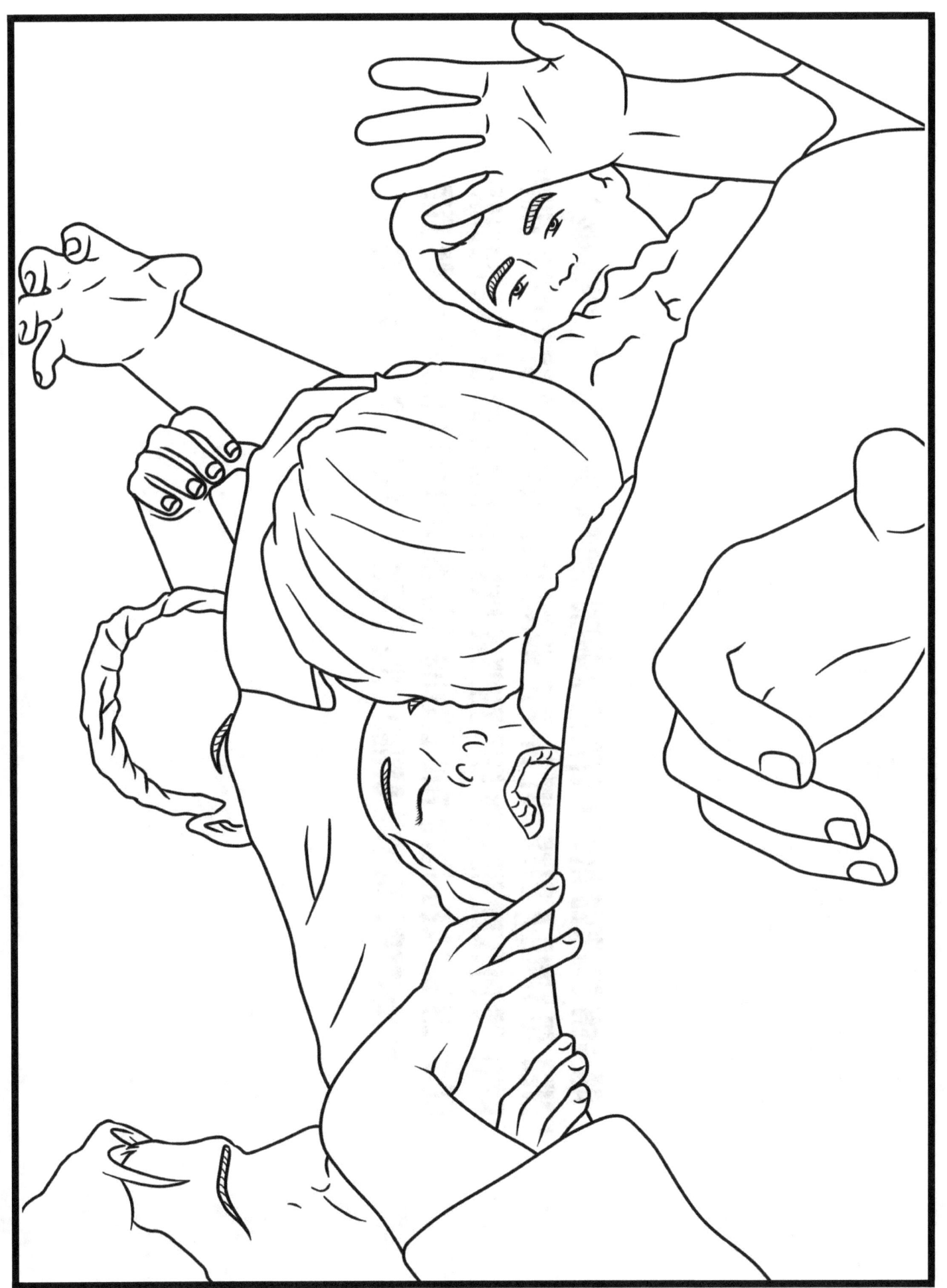

AS BEN BACKED AWAY LITTLE KAREN SNUCK UP FROM BEHIND AND TRIED TO TAKE A BITE OUT OF HIS ARM! BUT BEN WAS STRONGER THAN HER! HE PICKED HER UP AND THREW HER TO THE SIDE OF THE ROOM! HE THEN BACKED INTO THE CELLAR AND BARRICADED HIMSELF AS THE MONSTERS ON THE OTHER SIDE WERE FILLING UP THE HOUSE

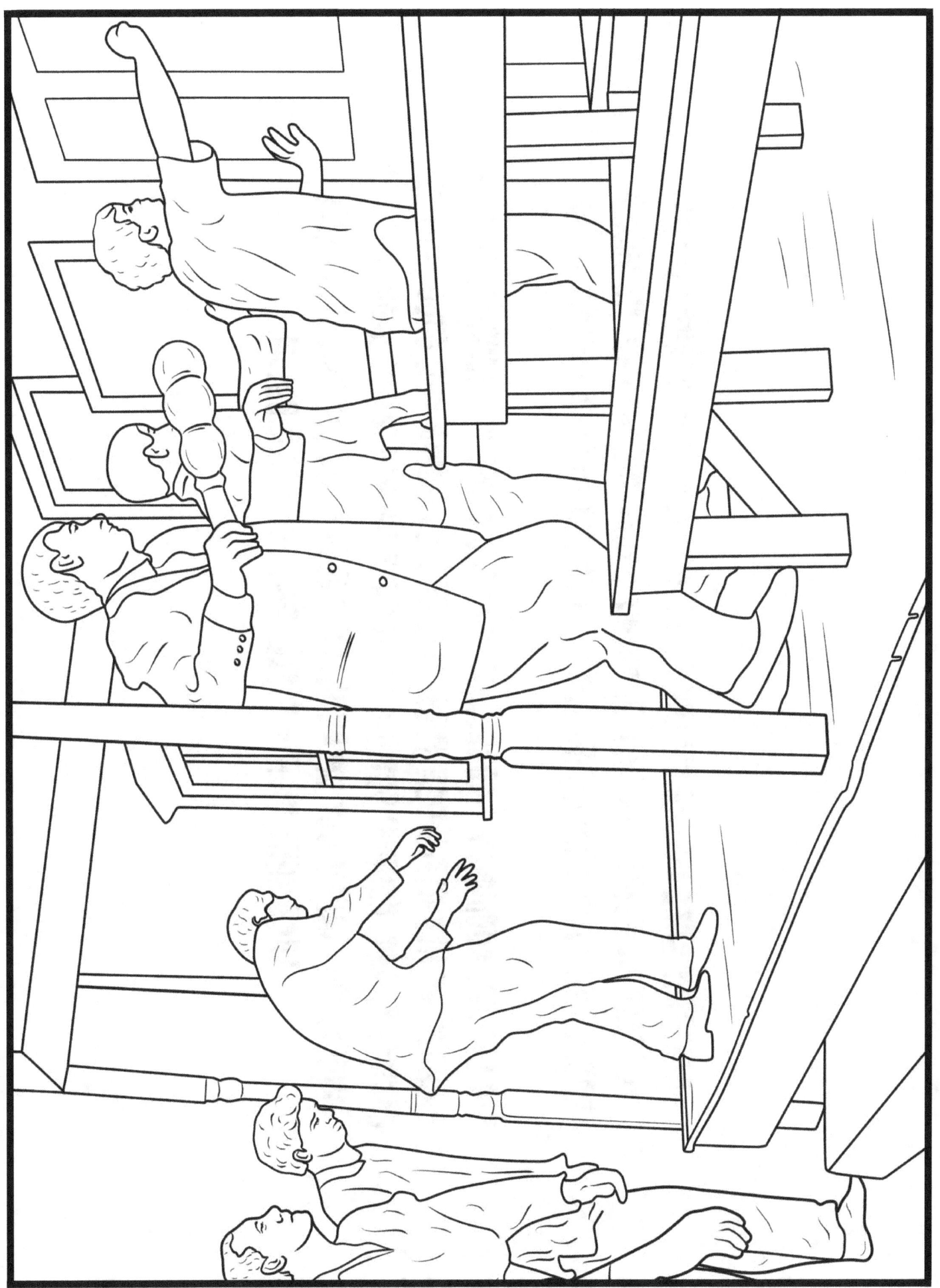

BEN FELT SAFE IN THE CELLAR AS HE GOT THE LAST BOARD PLACED
LOCKING HIMSELF INSIDE AND AWAY FROM THE DANGER. HE WENT
DOWN THE STAIRS AND SAW THE COOPERS BOTH DEAD ON THE FLOOR.

MR COOPER SUDDENLY AROSE, AND STARTED COMING TOWARDS BEN. IN
3 SHOTS OF HIS RIFLE BEN TOOK MR. COOPER DOWN FOR GOOD! BUT OF
COURSE IF MR. COOPER GOT UP, THEN THAT WOULD MEAN MRS. COOPER
WOULD PROBABLY GET UP AS WELL. INDEED SHE DID AND WITH ONE
LAST SHOT OF HIS RIFLE, BEN TOOK HER DOWN.

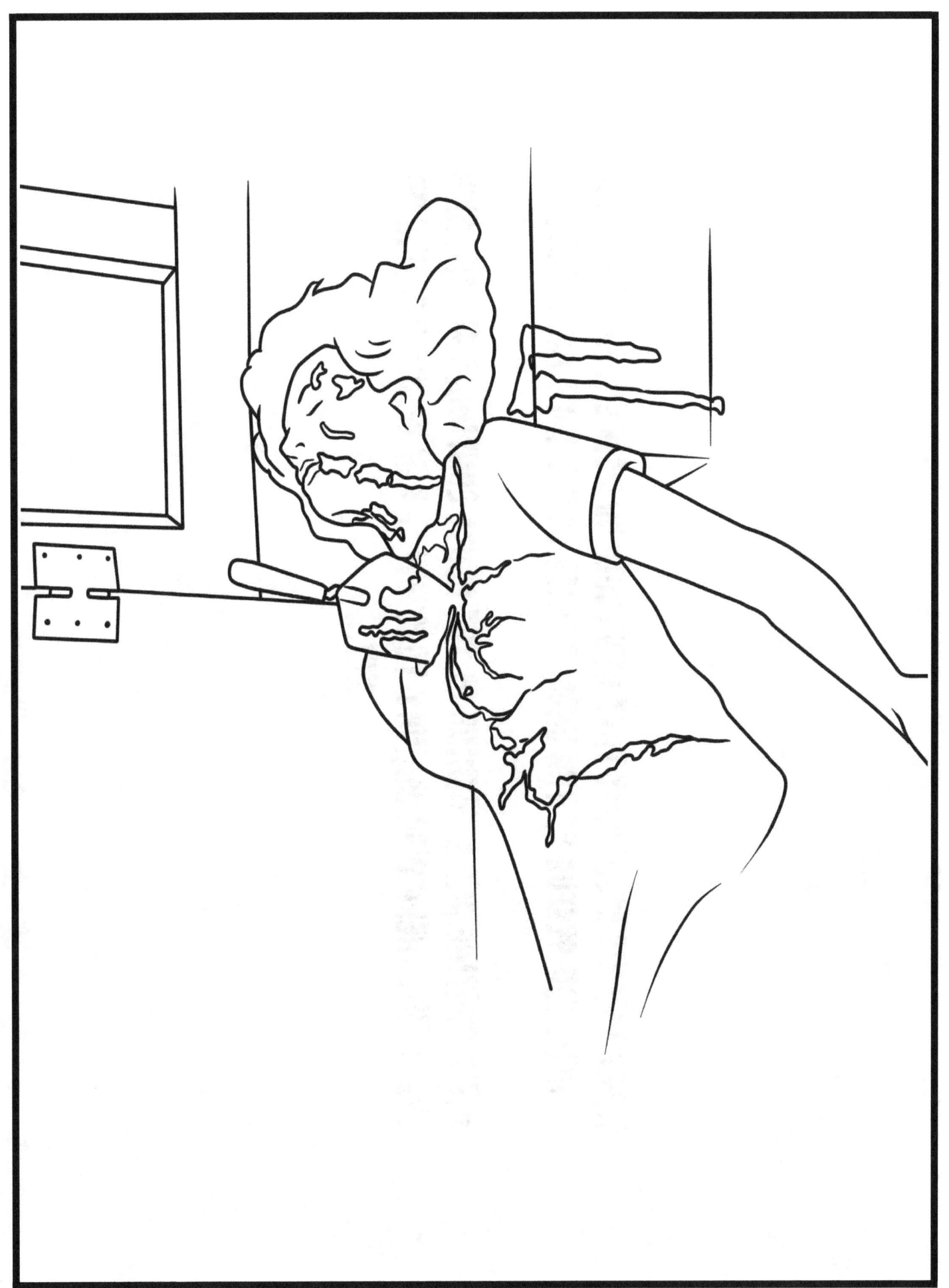

THERE WASN'T MUCH LEFT THAT BEN COULD DO NOW EXCEPT WAIT AND HOPE FOR RESCUE AS THE UNDEAD TRIED TO GET INTO THE CELLAR.

THEIR BEATING AND SMASHING OF THE HOUSE CONTINUED ALL THROUGH THE NIGHT. THERE WAS NO WAY TO KNOW IF BEN WOULD SURVIVE OR

NOT...

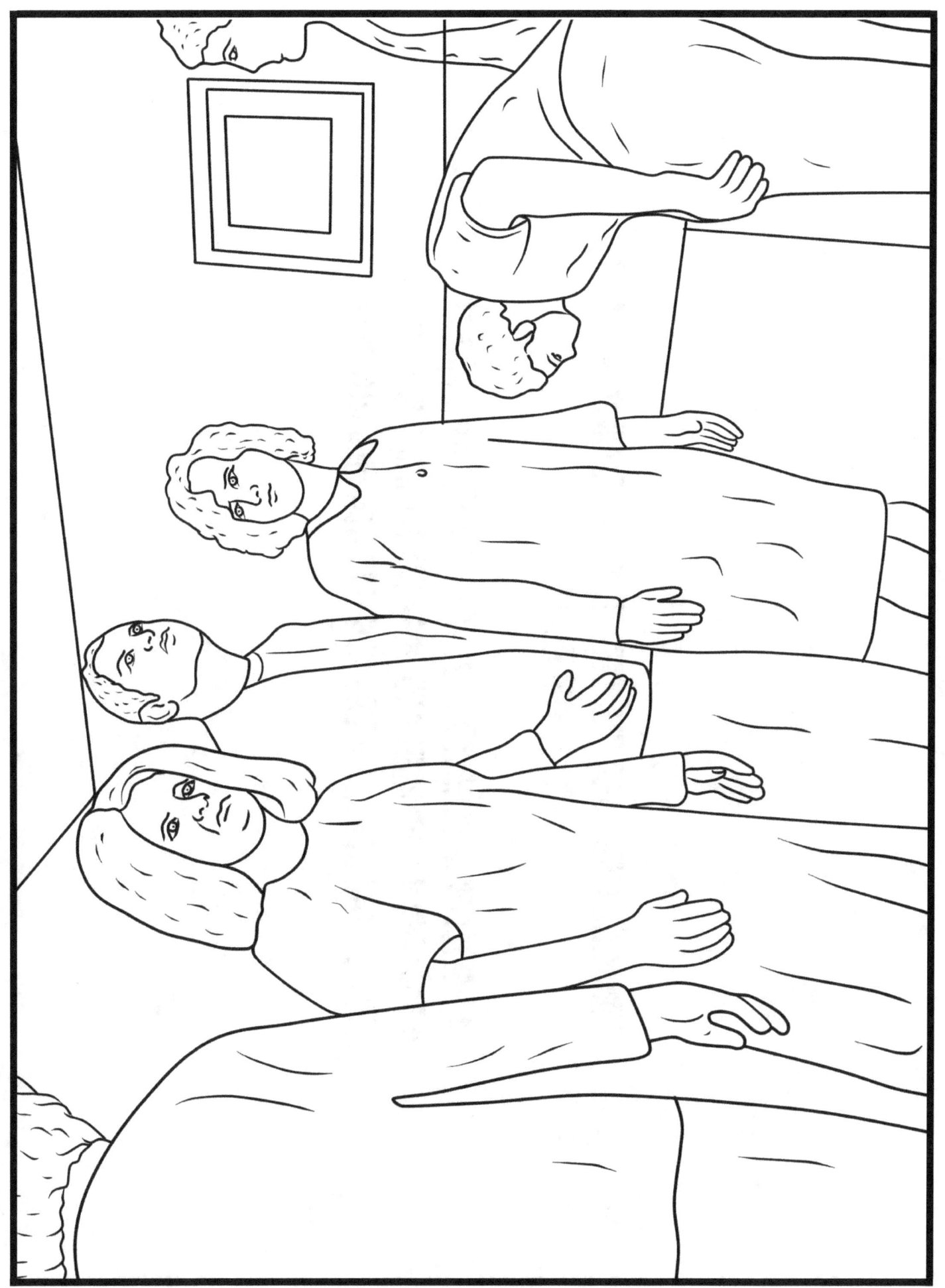

MORNING CAME AND ALL SEEMED TO BE A CALM QUIET AT THE HOUSE.

A HELICOPTER STARTED FLYING UP IN THE AIR, TOWARDS A LARGEGROUP OF MEN AND DOGS MARCHING TOWARDS THE AREA OF THE HOUSE WHERE BEN HAD BOARDED HIMSELF UP.

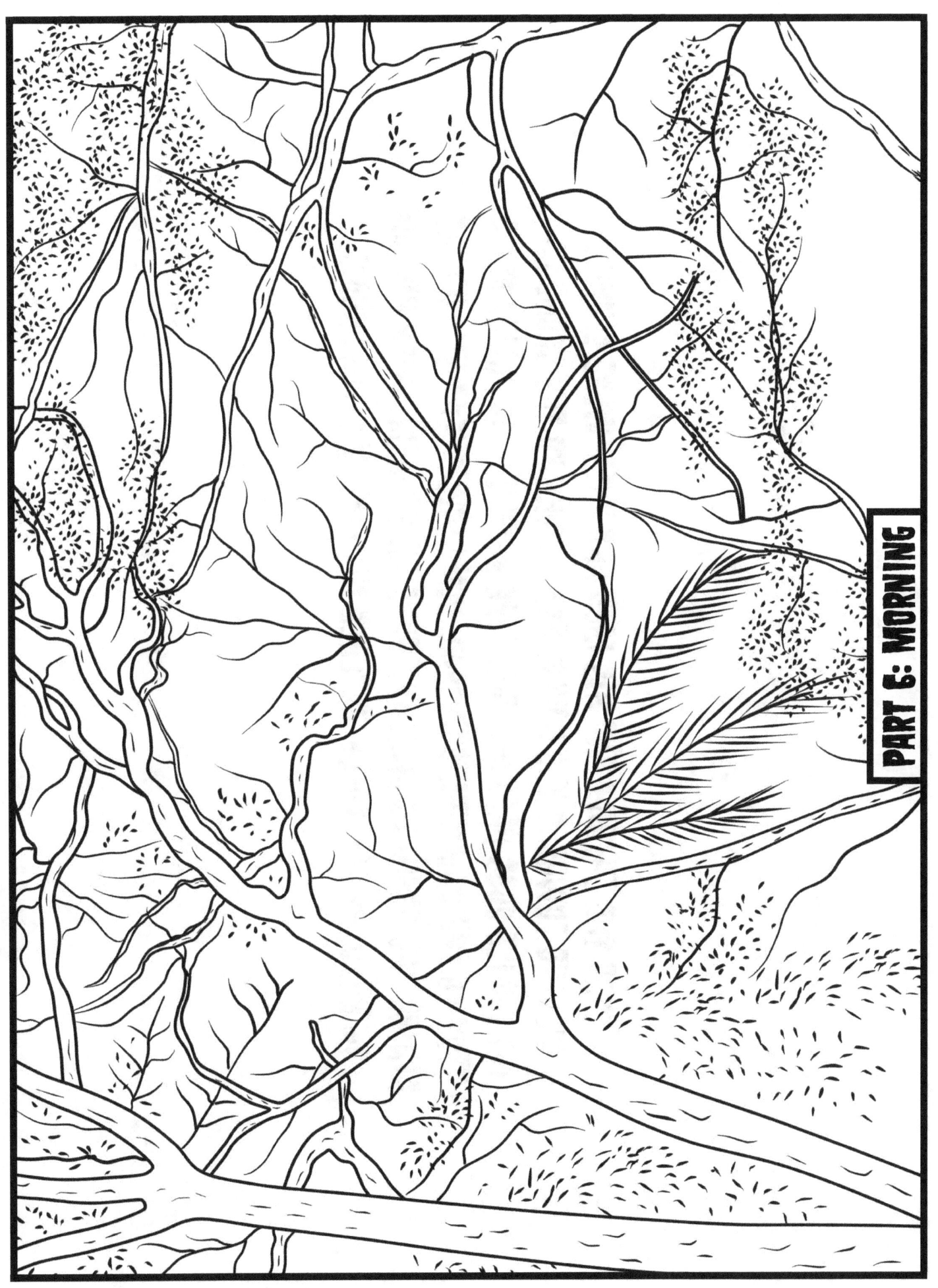

PART 6: MORNING

IT WAS THE SHERIFF AND HIS MEN AND THEY WERE SLOWLY MOVING TOWARDS THE HOUSE. BEN AWOKE TO THE SOUND OF THE POLICE DOGS BARKING. GUN FIRE RANG OUT AS POLICE PUT A STOP TO THE WANDERING UNDEAD. BEN SLOWLY CRAWLY UP THE STAIRS AND BEGIN TO OPEN THE BARRICADED DOOR. WITH HIS GUN IN HAND, HE CAREFULLY ENTERED THE EMPTY LIVING ROOM.

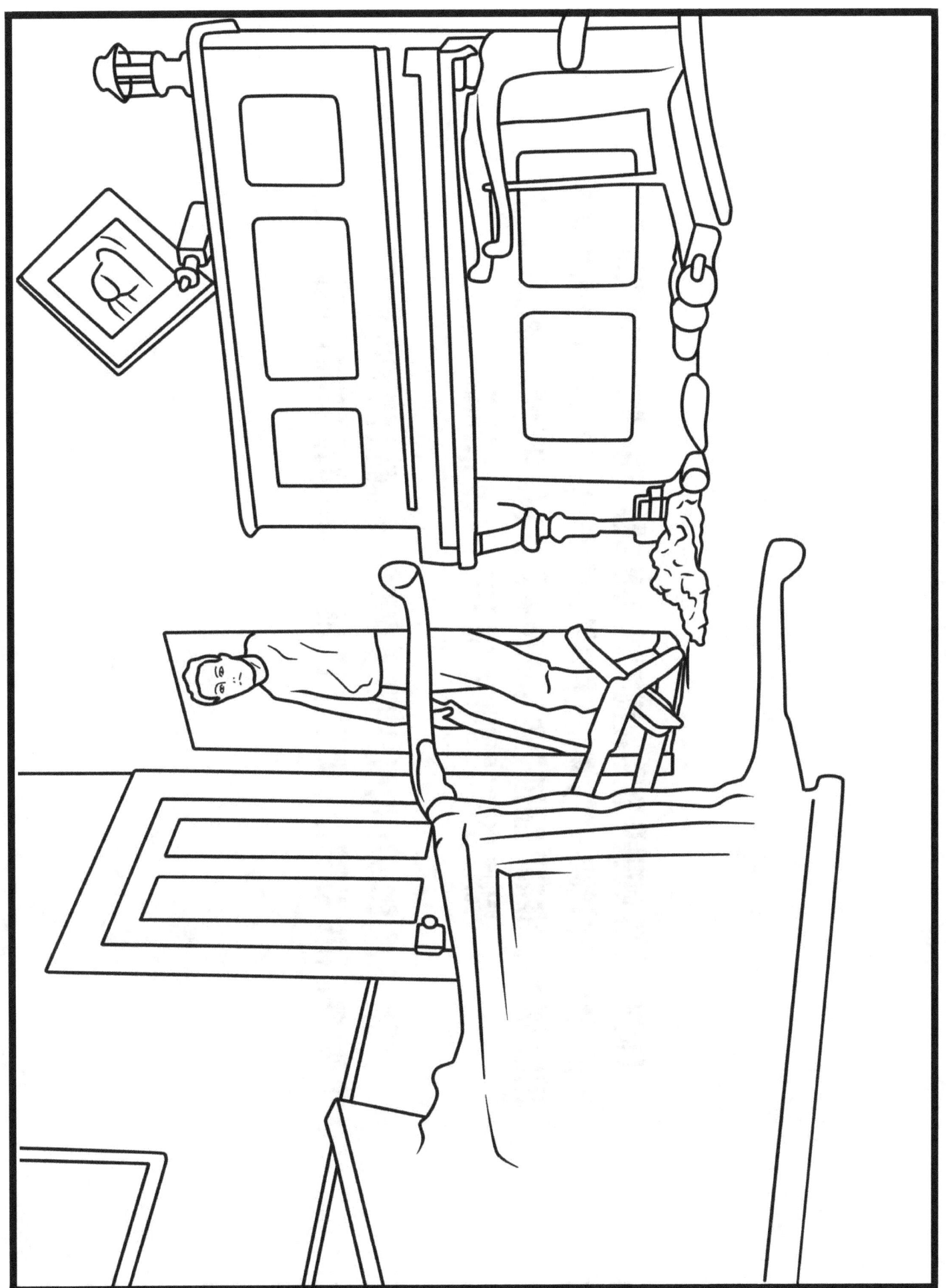

LOOKING THROUGH THE WINDOW BEN SAW THE MEN OUTSIDE. "I HEARD A NOISE" SAID ONE OF THE OFFICERS. "ALRIGHT VINCE HIT HIM IN THE HEAD" SAID THE SHERIFF AND WITH THAT, BANG!, BEN WAS SHOT SQUARE IN THE EYES....DEAD

"OK LETS GO GET HIM. THAT'S ANOTHER ONE FOR THE FIRE" ORDERED THE SHERIFF. AND IT IS HERE THAT OUR STORY ENDS.....

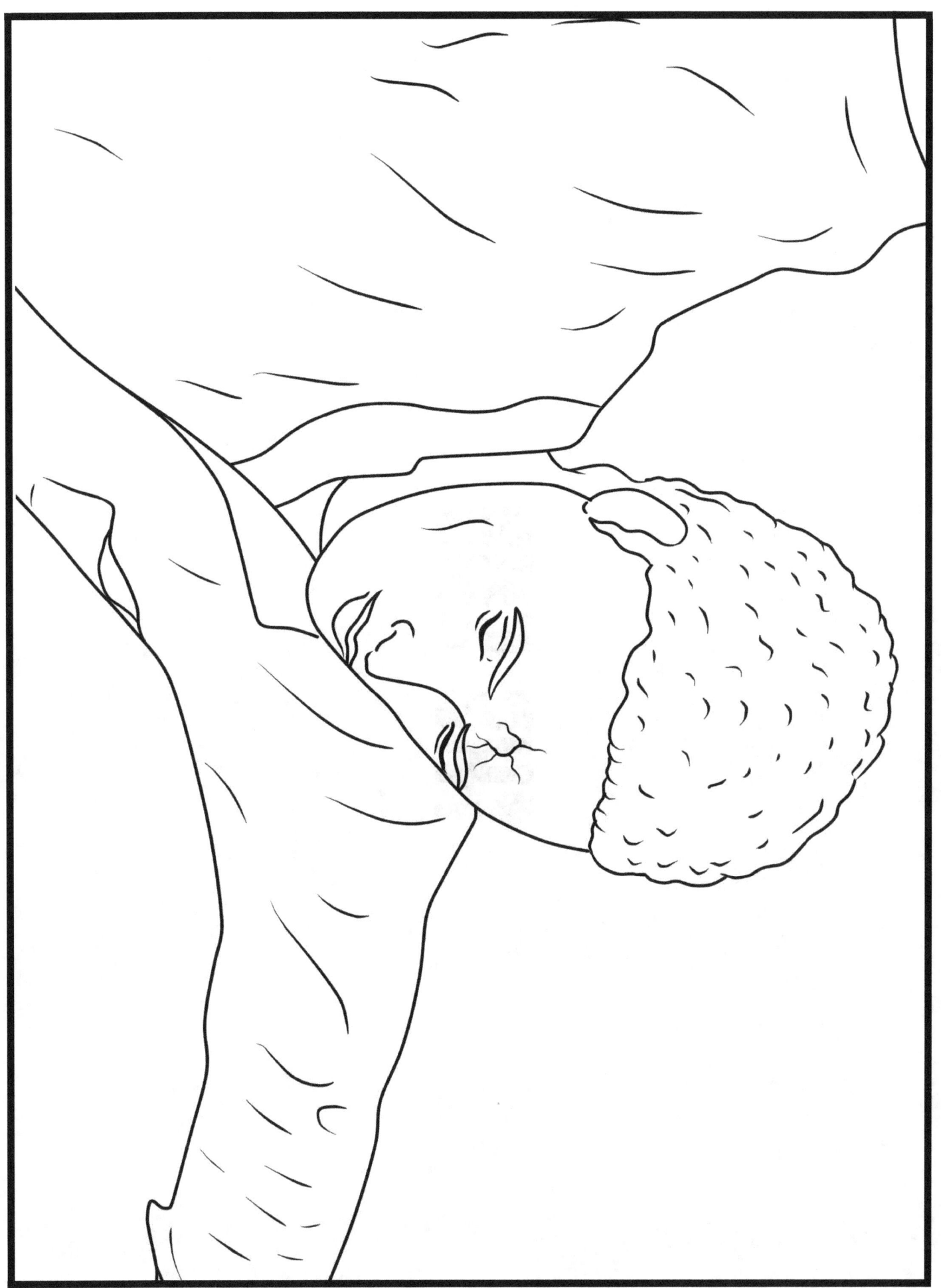

THE END

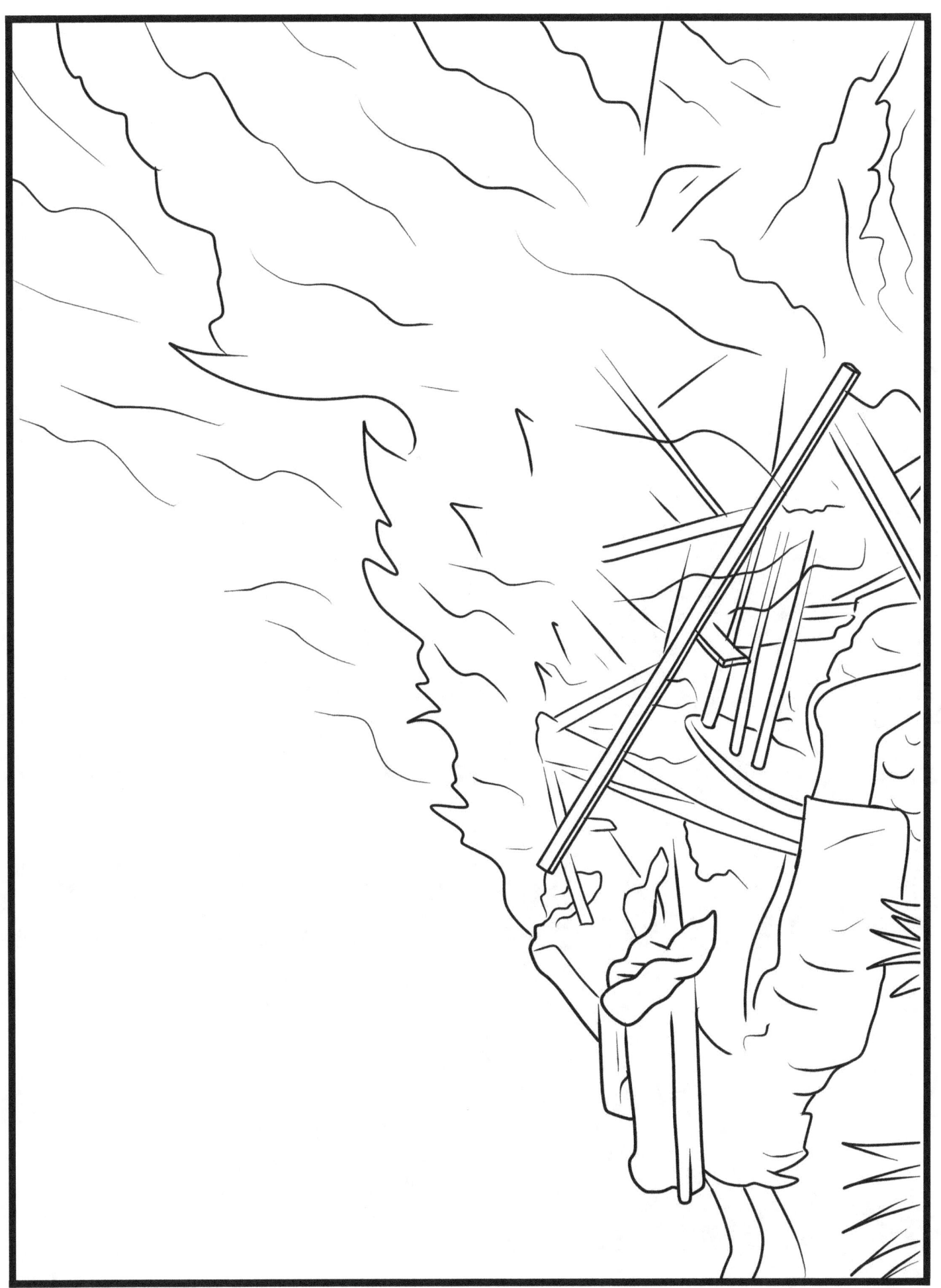

ABOUT THE AUTHOR

JORDAN COLTON IS AN AVID FAN OF HORROR & BAD MOVIES. THIS IS HIS FIRST COLORING BOOK, AND FELT NIGHT OF THE LVING DEAD WAS THE PERFECT CHOICE FOR A QUALITY COLORING BOOK.

HE CURRENTLY RESIDES IN UTAH WITH HIS CAT AND HORROR FILM COLLECTION.

YOU CAN LEARN MORE ABOUT HIS HORRID COLORING BOOKS AT:

WWW.HORRIDCOLORINGBOOKS.COM

USE THE PROMO CODE "BARBARA" FOR FREE SHIPPING IN THE US

ALSO CHECK OUT HIS OTHER COLORING BOOKS:

VOLUME 1: THE NIGHT OF THE LIVING DEAD
VOLUME 2: THE KRAMPUS
VOLUME 3: MANOS THE HANDS OF FATE

www.ingramcontent.com/pod-product-compliance
Lightning Source LLC
Chambersburg PA
CBHW081003170526
45158CB00010B/2886